The Amazing Presence of God

Time in God's Presence

Terrence Richards

Kingdom Publishers

Copyright© Terrence Richards 2025

All rights reserved. No part of this book may be reproduced in any form by photocopying or any electronic or mechanical means, including information storage or retrieval systems, without permission in writing from both the copyright owner and the publisher of the book. The right of Terrence Richards to be identified as the author of this work has been asserted by him in accordance with the Copyright, Designs, and Patents Act 1988 and any subsequent amendments thereto.

A catalogue record for this book is available from the British Library.

All Scripture quotations have been taken from the King James and New International versions of the bible.

ISBN: 978-1-916801-37-0

1st Edition 2025 by Kingdom Publishers, London, UK.

You can purchase copies of this book from any leading bookstore or at: **www.kingdompublishers.co.uk**

Thanks

To Nikki, my wife for her support over the years and for completing this work of God.

Contents

Introduction	9
Miracles on the Waters	15
A visitation in Jamaica	19
Surrey life	26
Bike waiting	29
Meeting my soul mate	32
My Salvation	36
The amazing presence of God	41
How to enter God's presence	58
The Tabernacle prayer	64
Jacob's time in God's presence	85
Being a witness at work	92
Coming out of comfort zone	99

Introduction

I believe that every person has a unique opportunity to enter into God's amazing presence, a holy time when you let the power of God transform you and direct your path for life. A place where only God Himself is magnified, He is a holy God, and says that He who worships Me must worship Me in spirit and in truth. It's not in our own strength.
One of the main keys is breaking through this natural world around us and everything that we see. Think for a moment, all your life you've been accustomed to taking things as our eyes see and interpret.

"While we look not at the things which are seen, but at the things which are not seen: for the things which are seen are temporal; but the things which are not seen are eternal."
2 Corinthians 4:18 (KJV)

I always thought the memories of someone are more powerful than them standing in front of you. Like Jesus, when He walked this earth in the flesh. He was great, and after His ascension to heaven, He is now greater.

Jesus said to His disciples, "When I ascend to the Father, I will send to you the Holy Spirit the unseen, who is able to do greater works than I."

On the Day of Pentecost, the disciples were in one accord, in perfect unity. Undivided, no strife, the presence of the Holy Spirit will not turn up in its fullness in disunity, the Holy Spirit came in fullness like an earthquake and mighty wind. All power and the presence of God were released upon the disciples, and then they started to speak in tongues. The greater works had started, and it was released after the ascension of Christ. The Bible says the veil in the great temple was torn in two, giving us full access to come into His wonderful presence – unlimited, without any restriction.

When the Lord spoke to Moses, He told Him to build Him a Tabernacle where He would come down and meet with His people. They had to follow a strict protocol to enter into God's presence. Only the chosen priest could enter, no person could just enter in. They would be struck down straight away and killed, by the awesome holy power of God.
Entering the Tabernacle the following was found:

- Sixty pillars surrounding the Tabernacle,
- A gate, where you could enter, and which was the only way in and out,
- Next, the Altar of Burnt Offering is straight in front of you,
- Then the Lavar,
- Following would be the Second Veil, which would lead to the House of Truth,
- Leading to the Third Veil, and the most holy place where the amazing glorified presence of God resided.

Many of us are trying to find God in our daily walk, but I believe it's God who has made provision and is in pursuit, to meet with us daily in the struggles of life. He is a true friend who shall stick closer than a brother

This proves to me that the unseen is more powerful than the seen. It's like the wind, you can't see it but you can certainly feel the effects. It's also like many famous artists, who died with not much appreciation for their work, yet after they died, their work became priceless.
It's all about letting go of our selfish needs and the work of the flesh.
Like in the book of John:
"Verily, verily, I say unto you, except a corn of wheat fall into the ground and die, it abideth alone: but if it die, it bringeth forth much fruit. He that

loveth his life shall lose it; and he that hateth his life in this world shall keep it unto life eternal."
John 12: 24-25 (KJV)

Our life in this Christian Walk is a process of dying. Paul, the Apostle says, *"I die daily to things of the flesh."* As we stay in God's presence, everyone has the opportunity for their life to grow fruit and prosper. I believe, that every day there is a battle raging for our minds because our minds control everything that we do. Our brain is like the electronic control unit (ECU) of a car, which controls airflow, fuel injectors' cycle, and ignition timing, also, protecting the engine from destroying itself.

The whole running of a vehicle depends on it functioning properly, so if there is a fault with the control unit, it would have a disastrous effect on the rest of the systems, depending on what it is. It's the same with our mind. The thing is the devil will never give up the fight for your mind. He wants to take control and influence your actions, and the things you do. He will do it in a way you won't even realize. The Bible says he is a liar, thief, and deceiver, from the beginning.

But through Jesus Christ, we have the victory because over two thousand years ago at Calvary, Jesus gave His life, so that we can have the victory through Him. The Roman soldiers mocked Him, spat in His face, and pulled His beard out...for real!

"I offered my back to those who beat me, my cheeks to those who pulled out my beard; I did not hide my face from mocking and spitting."
Isaiah 50:6 (NIV)

Then, they made a crown of thorns...Jewish thorns, which contained poison, and rammed it on His head. The spikes on it got soaked in His blood. The day before the crucifixion in the Garden of Gethsemane, the Lord Jesus experienced anguish, a severe mental torment. If you've ever experienced a stressful day at work, it's nothing compared to what Jesus experienced that night. The Bible says that night, His sweat was as blood.

There was a serious battle going on in His mind, good against evil. The flesh, the carnal side of man, against the spirit. This tells me that when the evil one comes to attack you in your mind, with evil thoughts and things that do not glorify God, you just have to bring down every thought captive under subjection and soak it in that supernatural blood.

"Casting down imaginations, and every high thing that exalteth itself against the knowledge of God, and bringing into captivity every thought to the obedience of Christ."
2 Corinthians 10:5 (KJV)

"You are so amazing, Lord, I could shout it from the highest mountain and give You praise."

The Lord has paid the price to redeem what was lost, and bring us back into His presence, and is the main reason I wrote this book.
Mary, the mother of Jesus, in order to conceive a baby, needed her egg to be fertilised by a man. In Mary's case, there was no man involved, it was supernatural. His DNA came from heaven and God the Father. His precious blood shed on the cross was redemption to wash away our sins and pain. More of all, to bring us back into His presence, so we can be free in our minds, and receive the peace of God. Every day brings on new challenges, so keep persevering because we are in a battle, but operating from a place of victory, and because of the finished work of Jesus on the cross, just never give up.

"Thou wilt shew me the path of life: In thy presence is fullness of joy."
Psalm 16:11 (KJV)
In this book, is my story and the caption of my life. Some of the things I've been through and experiences. Growing up from a kid and looking back

now, I still see the hand of God at work in my life, even when I did not care about serving God. His love and mercies were always there, even through all the troubles life threw at me. You will also hear about miracles on the waters when my family nearly died at sea going to Jamaica from England, and a visitation in Jamaica I could never forget, meeting my soulmate. Also, about a life-transforming supernatural time when I *spent time in God's Amazing presence* and how I came to know the Lord. You will also hear about how I got saved, and when I made my first real-life-changing prayer to the Father. You will read about powerful keys to put in action on how you can enter into God's presence on a daily basis.

Artwork by Terrence Richards

Miracles on the Waters

This all started in 1966, as my mum, Leanora told me about her experience of how her life got transformed and saved by the Lord, and she became a born-again Christian. She was at work one day when her friend invited her to come along to an AA Alan evangelistic crusade meeting, which was held in Tooting, South London. My mum and her friend also brought along her sick sister, who was in desperate need of healing.

They all jumped on the bus from Addiscombe to Tooting, as it was the last day of the crusade. She said as they entered the meeting, she could feel the difference in the atmosphere; it was amazing. It was charged with the presence of God, and it was great to be there. It felt like nothing she had ever experienced before. I just think it was so glorious when the Lord could have you be in the right place at the right time. The message that the preacher spoke on was a man's life that was like the flower of the field, referencing Isaiah.

"The voice said, Cry. And he said, What shall I cry? All flesh is grass, and all the goodliness thereof is as the flower of the field: the grass withereth, the flower fadeth: because the spirit of the LORD bloweth upon it: surely the people is grass. The grass withereth, the flower fadeth: but the Word of our God shall stand forever.'"
Isaiah 40:6-8 (KJV)

My mum said as he said this, he threw a bunch of flowers across the stage, then gave an altar call, and they all responded and went up, my mum, her sister and her friend. They received a miracle of salvation, and her friend got healed. That night, they all gave their life and committed to the Lord. A transforming evening and remarkable, my mum said.

By Monday, she was already a witness at work, spreading the good news to her work colleagues and anyone willing to hear the transforming word of God. In 1969, the Lord spoke to Mum to go back to Jamaica for a holiday and have an open-air service. She managed to make provisions and worked hard to make it happen, arriving in Jamaica. My parents stayed at her parent's house and they said it was ok to hold a meeting in their large front garden, as they had the space.

She gave the Word of God to the local people and told them about His love. Many people received it with gladness, and some people stepped out in faith, receiving miracle healing. In the end, it worked out very well. Many people came to know the Lord through the words she preached and the spirit of God at work.

She vowed to the Lord to return one day to live here permanently and start a church. Mum returned to family life in England, bringing up six children, which had its ups and downs, but each day, trusting in the Lord that one day she would return to Jamaica.

Keeping faith alive, my dad, Joseph worked very hard and saved enough money. He returned to Jamaica, acquired the land, and built our new five-bedroom house for us all to live in, just down the road from my grandparents. In 1974, all our belongings were shipped to Kitson Town in Jamaica. It was September 1974, and winter was setting in. I was only four years old but still remember some of the experiences. My dad decided we would travel by boat to Jamaica and not fly from Gatwick airport. I had five other brothers and sisters travelling, including my parents. The boat was called Begona, it was a Spanish vessel.

On arrival, plenty of other families were taking the trip as well, and as we left port everything was fine. Three days into the journey, we arrived in Spain. Everyone had the chance to get off the boat, to do sightseeing, shopping and so forth. The next port of call was Venezuela from Tenerife.

Days into sailing, there were engine problems and a fire, which was put out, but the engines could not restart. The boat started to take on water and listed. It was very scary, and things on the ship started to fall over. Even as a young boy, I still remember some of the things that happened. Being a large family, my mum was busy and trying to help everyone. Her biggest concern was my younger sister, Alice, who was only one year old. We were placed on the lower decks of the ship, and when the engines finally gave up, there was a loud noise and panic. My mum was worried for us all and started to pray to God for a miracle, to deliver us from this situation and protect her family.

No one knew what was going on, and I remember the water coming into the cabin, and my feet were getting wet. The air conditioning stopped working and started to get very hot. I tried looking out of the window, but it was all misted up. We took out our belongings to the upper deck just like other families, and there was chaos with people shouting, being upset, etc. On the upper deck, it was cooler, but we were adrift with no power. Mum had a hard time looking after us all due to the poor sanitation. My sister Alice was very sick as she was still taking the bottle. Mum went to the canteen to try to get help from members of staff, for food or water for her children. They had to make a manual fire, due to no power, just to heat my sister's milk. She did her best to keep her baby alive. The situation was getting more and more desperate.

The captain sent an 'SOS' out, but the tugboat was miles away and couldn't reach us for at least 24 hours. It was called the Oceanic, and it was a miracle we did not sink. Praise You, Lord, You are so amazing. The tugboat would not tow us to La Guairá or Kingston, as all the passengers would have to be put in quarantine, as there was a high risk of disease. Instead, they intended to tow us to Barbados, where no quarantine was issued. Everyone thought we were going to die and felt like we were on the Titanic. When the tugboat arrived, the children were given food to much relief, but my sister was still poorly. It took another three days of towing to reach Barbados. When we eventually arrived, we were all so relieved, and Mum thanked God for a miracle. She gave Him all the glory and honour. In Barbados, flights were arranged to go to various destinations.

I believe it took another few days to clear all the passengers from the boat. There were news crews everywhere, interviewing passengers. My half-sister at home in England saw us on the news. We eventually arrived in Jamaica. I thank God for the miracles on the waters, that saved us and that He sent His angels to keep us afloat.

A visitation in Jamaica

We, the family, eventually arrived in Jamaica after ten long days later at sea. My dad, Joseph had previously gone over and had the house built, it was a five-bedroom bungalow with lots of land and space, a big driveway with iron gates up front. I was still a toddler and have great memories of living in Jamaica, especially the lovely hot weather we woke up to every morning. On the land where we had our house built, there were many fruit trees. To the right of the house was a huge mango tree, and at the back of the house, there were pear, ackee and apple trees.

My sisters and I would climb the trees when Mum and Dad weren't looking. One day, I decided to climb the mango tree because I noticed there was the most beautiful bird I've ever seen. I think it was a parakeet with many colours in its feathers. The only thing was, it was quite high up in the branches of the tree. I did not let that deter me, so I climbed up the tree and decided to stroke it like a cat. Big mistake! It went for me and nearly took my hand off, pain like I have never experienced. His beak sank into my little fingers, and I screamed out loud, probably the whole neighbourhood heard me. Mum came running out with my sisters to see if I was okay. I then nearly fell out of the tree with shock. Blood was pouring everywhere from my hand. I must say that was the last time I ever tried to stroke a parakeet. They are nice to look at, but can be deadly if handled incorrectly.

My brothers, sisters and I were also given chores to do, and one of them was to sweep the veranda and polish it. We used to make it fun by climbing into an old crocus bag. My two sisters had to sit in it, and we dragged them around to shine the floor. I would spin them around till I went dizzy, then let them go, and watch the bag go shooting off like a missile across the floor. We had so much fun, we didn't need much money or possessions to have fun, and we always found something to do. Another game we used to play was called Rollover. Three of us would lie on the bed and 'steamroll' each person lying next to them. While you were doing so, you shouted, "Roll over", and the first to fall off the bed would lose.

Every Sunday, my mum would encourage us to put on our best clothes to go to Sunday school. I looked forward to going every week. We would learn about stories from the Bible, from Adam and Eve, to David and Goliath, and of stories of Jesus healing the sick. Yet, this Sunday started off a little differently.

We even had two dogs at the time, Bulrush and Fire-rocket. I remember a story. It was a sunny Sunday morning, before church. The normal procedures were that we would all usually have breakfast and get ready. In England, people with dogs would normally leave them in the house when going out. In Jamaica, it's the other way around. Everyone would leave them outside till they came back. I led Fire-rocket outside as normal, and Bulrush would normally be okay with that. She would just chill outside, get up to mischief, or just hang out with other dogs and do what they would normally do. As I used to spend a lot of time with her, when my dad said it was time to leave, I said to Bulrush, "Come on time to go outside." Despite my best efforts, calling her, trying to lift her, she was not having it. she had made up her mind to stay in the house. I was worried thought she might need the vet. My dad was calling me again to leave, so I gave up and decided to leave her in the house. Whilst we were out, I was a little apprehensive hoping Bulrush was ok. To our surprise when we got back home, Bulrush had given birth to five lovely puppies. Ahh, no matter the cost, Bulrush did not want to have her puppies outside, amazing.

I remember also going to school in Jamaica. It was not like schools in England; it was very strict. The teachers would walk around the classroom with a cane in their hands and ask you a question about the lesson. If you did not know the answer or were messing around in class or daydreaming, you would feel the sharp pain of the cane connecting with your body. Hence, I always paid attention in class except this one time I was playing drums on my desk, daydreaming, I was in a music band. All of a sudden, I felt this hot sting on my neck! I thought it was a bee sting, but it was the cane. Ouch, ouch, ouch! When I was five, I had an experience I will never forget. It made me think about the supernatural world around us.

My cousin Tyrone, who was in his mid-20s, often visited us and sometimes borrowed my dad's van. He was extremely close to my younger sister. They would often spend a lot of time playing together and enjoying each other's company, which made it even more sad. One day, my mother gathered us all around to inform us of the tragic news that our cousin Tyrone had been killed. It was said he was involved in a bad company, which cost him his life. We all took this hard and dealt with it in our own ways. I still have fond memories of him, and I was only five when he died. A month after he died I couldn't sleep one night so I got up to get a drink from the kitchen. When I passed my sister's room on the way back, I saw her sitting up in bed talking to someone. Well, at first, I thought she was sleep-talking as there was no one else in the room. I entered her room and asked her who she was talking to, and she replied she was talking to Tyrone, and that he was standing at the end of her bed dressed in white, asking her to come and play.

I couldn't see him, but I certainly felt the presence of someone else in the room. I was scared, so I went running and screaming to wake up my mum. Looking back now, she said just before I came into her room, she was having a vision of Tyrone being in the house. So, it was no surprise when I went screaming into her room. My mum had been a Christian and filled with the Holy Spirit of God for many years. As she walked into my sister's bedroom, she could see him in the spirit, speaking to my sister. Realising that it was my cousin, she spoke in tongues and rebuked him to leave the house right then in the name of Jesus. My Mum explained it was a familiar spirit that had no rest after death. So, my mum continued firmly and confidently, and I could see her marching him out of the house, down across the veranda, all the way down the driveway. She continued to march the spirit down the road in the night, out of sight, back to his place of rest.

I still remember her saying, "In the name of Jesus, leave this house." I watched my mum march him out of the house and down the street. This was all happening in the early hours of the morning, around 2 am. All I could hear were the mosquitoes in the bushes, and the moon shone so bright that night, it felt like daytime, but at night! I tell you this, he never came back! It was an experience to remember, and this opened up my mind to realize that there is a spirit world around us, whether we believe it or not. It's like the air we breathe, you can't see it, but can feel and see the effects of it around us.

"...And it is appointed unto men once to die, but after this the judgment:"
Hebrews 9:27 (KJV)

This seems to me that once the spirit has left the body, there is no coming back until you meet the Lord in judgment. So my cousin was a familiar spirit sent from the underworld to entice my sister. I believe the spirits on this earth need a body to operate in, and that's why Adam and Eve were given a body, and why Satan transformed himself into a serpent. He could not come back in his natural form because he would get rejected.

"Thine heart was lifted up because of thy beauty, thou hast corrupted thy wisdom by reason of thy brightness: I will cast thee to the ground, I will lay thee before kings, that they may behold thee."
Ezekiel 28:17 (KJV)

He was cast to the ground and rejected by God. He took the form of a snake so when he saw Adam and Eve, he was looking at what he lost, authority and power. I believe this is why my mum rebuked my cousin in the spirit, back to his place of rest, because he was an evil familiar spirit. Familiar spirits can impersonate people, and they need a body to operate on earth, and it was illegal, not having any right to be at our house. There were many times in the Bible when Jesus rebuked an evil spirit to come out. Here is an example of this.

"And when he went forth to land, there met him out of the city a certain man, which had devils long time, and ware no clothes, neither abode in any house, but in the tombs.
28 When he saw Jesus, he cried out, and fell down before him, and with a loud voice said, What have I to do with thee, Jesus, thou Son of God most high? I beseech thee, torment me not.
29 (For he had commanded the unclean spirit to come out of the man. For oftentimes it had caught Him: and he was kept bound with chains and fetters; and he brake the bands, and was driven of the devil into the wilderness.)"
Luke 8:27-29 (KJV)

Let's take a deeper look at this. As Jesus stepped onto land, He was met by a man possessed by demon spirits. These demon spirits can control territories and have a stronghold if we let them. I believe that every land and place we go and place our feet on, we should take authority over evil spirits in Jesus' Name. It says they were there for a long time, and they tormented and terrorised the people and the town in such a bad way. The man could not dwell in the community he lived in; he lived in the tombs.

The demons recognised he was Jesus, the son of the Most High God. What a powerful thing when we can be recognised because of the shed blood of Jesus on us. I believe in the spirit, the Glory of God rests on believers. We have been given authority over all principalities and power. We can only do this through walking in the spirit, not in the flesh. The flesh brings no glory to God.

"But the hour cometh, and now is, when the true worshippers shall worship the Father in spirit and in truth: for the Father seeketh such to worship him."
John 4:23 (KJV)

Jesus said He sought true worshipers who would worship Him in spirit and in truth. So, as we walk in the spirit, we will recognise the true words spoken by God and, more of all, it will bring you into Truth, in the amazing presence of God.

The Sanhedrin, the Jewish leaders of the synagogues or the church of its time, did not recognise Jesus standing in front of them, but the demons did. Therefore, every day when we wake up, we should seek the Lord in prayer and stay there till we get a breakthrough and transition from the flesh to the spirit. It's never easy to just stay till you get a breakthrough. You have to be determined like Jesus in the Garden of Gethsemane. His flesh did not want to go to the cross. The next day, He was dreading it for the flesh brings fear and torment to our souls. But He persevered and hit a breakthrough during the night, and that's when the Cross was won...that night, in the Garden.

There was a transition from the flesh to the spirit, praise God. The spirit in Him spoke and said, "Not my will but thy will be done." The Holy Spirit gives us the power to face opposition, defeat and evil power coming against us. It could be problems at work, at home or in our relationship with finances. No matter what, we have the authority through the Spirit over it. Praise God. Just like Jesus gave the commandment to the demon-possessed man to come out of him. We, in the same way, have to speak to problems to move. If you have faith like a mustard seed, you can speak to the mountain and it has to move.

Back to the story. "What is thy name?" Jesus said to the demon-possessed man. "Legion," the demon replied, as there were around 6000 demons present in that one man. They begged Jesus not to cast them to the bottomless pit or the deep, and they requested to go into the pigs. The demons then ran violently off the cliff and drowned.

This also shows me that evil spirits have the ability to come in and control a life if we don't have the shed blood of Jesus on our lives. If we live a life without Christ, it's an open door, because the enemy never gives up. He is constantly trying to fill our minds with negative thoughts and things that do not bring glory to God. The question is, what are you doing about it!! You need Christ to fight for you because the battle is the Lord's. When some problems in life seem overwhelming and you can't see your way out, just remember the following:

The battle is the Lord's
There is more for you than against you
You are operating from a place of victory, amen
So, we as a family continued living in sunny Jamaica till I was seven years old. My parents then decided life would be better if we moved back to England. Only this time, not by boat, but via airplane, and we had our tickets booked for British Airways.

Surrey life

Returning from Jamaica to England felt like making a U-turn in life, but I was happy about the experience. We had already sold our previous house in the UK, and we had to make a fresh start again. Getting onto the plane, I even remember what I was wearing - a navy blue and white matching outfit, feeling cool for the journey.
It was a long flight, about ten hours, which I spent watching cartoons, in-flight movies and playing with my toy cars. Because I love music, and no MP3 was available in those days, I pretended to play the drums on the side, and everywhere I went, I was always full of joy.

When we landed at Gatwick airport and the doors opened, I could feel the cold air hit my face, something that I wasn't used to for the last four years. I must say it was freezing. It was late September and the start of Autumn. When we arrived back in England, we just had temporary living accommodation in Addiscombe in Surrey, a three-bedroom house with five children and two adults. It was a nightmare, and luckily enough, this did not last long before moving to a town called New Addington, Surrey. It was a classic time in my childhood to remember, the house was much larger than a three-bedroom property, and it resembled a popular soap program on TV at the time.

I shared a bedroom with my two brothers, while my two sisters shared the other bedroom. It wasn't long after I started school, I was nine years old, and it was hard settling in. I remember a story that happened in my new Junior school. For comfort I used to suck my two fingers in my mouth, I was doing that on the first day when the teacher singled me out, and accused me of copying another pupil doing this. When she left the other child in class sucking his finger alone, for a second it felt worse than Jamaica. The teacher probably felt my face did not fit. But I persevered with school and meeting new friends. It took a while, but soon we settled into British life again. There were certain words that were different in the UK than in Jamaica, for example, the word 'film', I used to say 'flim'. Silly things like that were the way I was taught, but once I settled in, I enjoyed school and had lots of friends.

One good thing about Addington, it was a built-up new estate off the main road. So, growing up, I just saw it as a big playground with lots of alleyways and routes to disappear down, while getting up to mischief, chasing my sisters, and messing around. Just to the left of us were the woods, with acres of forest land and more places to play and hang out, which nearly landed me in trouble. One day, I came home from school, which was only about a ten-minute walk from our house. As I walked in, my Mum was cooking up dinner in the kitchen. I got changed and went out to play in the woods, the forbidden place my mum would always tell me to stay away from, but I never paid any notice! Just ahead of me, it looked like a small amount of smoke coming up from the ground. As I came closer, I realised someone had started a fire, which was smouldering. I thought to do a good thing and try to extinguish it. I tried my best, but was not sure it would not flare back up again, as there was still smoke ascending.

Then I ran home really quickly, just to find my younger sister had just gotten home from school. I was not sure the fire was out, so I decided to ring the Emergency Service. The operator, a nice lady on the phone, asked, "Can I help you? What service do you require?" At this point, my heart started beating fast. "Fireman," I said just as my sister entered the room, asking, "Who are you speaking to?" "No one," I said and slammed the phone down, because I thought she was going tell my mum. I was on the phone, then thought to myself, "I did not give my address, how will they find me?"

I felt elusive, my sister looked at me and said, "What are you smiling about?" "Nothing," I answered and dismissed the matter, going off to have my dinner. Halfway through eating, there was a loud knock at the door…bang, bang, bang. Oh no, who could that be? It was the fireman. But how did they find me? My mum said in a loud voice, "Who called the fireman out?" "Terrence?" When I heard my name, I just wanted the ground to open up and swallow me up.

"Did you do it?" In a quiet voice, I answered, "Yes." Very nervous, as I felt very intimidated with three large firemen standing at the door, I asked, "How did you find my address?" They answered that they have a call trace system, stating that even if someone hung up, they could trace where they lived. "Where's the fire?" he said, and I thought to myself that it was probably out by then, but I answered that it was in the woods. So, with the whole family watching me, I got my coat to lead them out to the woods where the suspected fire was. It felt like the longest walk of my life. When we got there, there was little smouldering and smoke left. I felt a bit better seeing that. The fireman just kicked it with his big boots and applied what was necessary to extinguish the fire, thank the Lord.

"Is that it?" he said. "Yes," I answered, and as I was not hanging around for any more conversation, I ran back to the house. I remember feeling a sense of duty and was happy to help.

History of New Addington rumored that the royal family, like King Henry the Eighth, many years ago when it was all a woodland area, hunted in the area and therefore the many roads are named after the royal family, like King Henry's Drive, and so on

Bike waiting

In those days, I thank God for my mum, Leanora, she was so loving and caring. It could not have been easy bringing up six kids. At the time, we had a new addition to the family, my baby sister. Mum always went the extra mile, as I reminisce back in Jamaica. For our birthdays, she would always make an effort to make us feel special and loved. I'm so grateful, whether it was a homemade birthday cake or fritters, or a nice present, we could count it all joy. There are lots of children in the world brought up with neglect, or unloved, and some don't even celebrate birthdays. It makes me very grateful for the things I have, thank God.

Must say that out of all the toys I've had, I always desired to have my own bicycle. I felt a bit left out, and every day after school, I saw the rest of my friends on their bikes. So, I kept asking my mum, "Will you buy me a bike, please?" I was relentless in my asking till one week she said, "Okay, I will get it for your birthday. I could not believe my ears. Yes, yes, yeah! I was overwhelmed with joy. I thought I was going to own my first bike, wow, love you mum.

I looked up to heaven and said, "Thank you, Lord, you are the greatest." Since it was for my birthday coming up in June, and it was only April, I thought it was still a long wait. But I received it in faith by the Word, she said. Instead of getting one from the shops because money was tight, she gave me her home shopping catalogue, which had a large section on bicycles to choose from. Which bike to choose, there were all different styles of bikes. The Chopper, to me, seemed like the only one to go, the only problem was the size in frame - too large for my size, what a shame!

So, I chose its younger brother, the Tomahawk. It was a perfect fit, red and blue with black writing down the middle of the frame. Awesome, I thought it looked amazing. I felt so blessed.

Unfortunately, the only thing with catalogue orders was that it could take up to four weeks to arrive.
So, every day I would come home from school with anticipation. The only thing on my mind was if my bike had come yet. I kept asking Mum as she was cooking up some food. "Not yet, son." This went on, week in and week out, day after day, same thing. After four weeks had passed, I could not bear the wait any longer, it was unbearable.

I asked my mum to ring up the company to find out why it was taking so long. They said there were weeks of delays on the item. At that stage, I was getting fed up with the whole situation. I started a new week at school, and there was only a week left until my birthday. By Wednesday, I had come to the end of my waiting. I had a tiring day, and the bike was not on my mind when I got home from school. As I opened the front door, to my amazement, there was this huge brown box under the stairs, taking up most of the room. I thought this had to be it, the long wait was over. It was my new bike and it had finally arrived after a five-week wait. I was so excited that I tore the package open to reveal my shiny new Tomahawk. I was out on it that same day, up and down, and I loved it, thanks, Mum.

Growing up, I always had a keen interest in engineering, it fascinated me how engines worked. To further this, I went to college to study motor vehicle engineering. I just wanted to learn how it all works, so I started to work in engineering. But I always felt in my heart I was called to do more than this. Deep in my heart, I always felt this calling and fire for the Lord to do something great one day.

"For I know the plans that I have for you, declares the Lord, plans to prosper you and not to harm you, plans to give you hope and a future."
Jeremiah 29:11 (NIV)

So, I believe no matter what job you're doing at the moment, if you love the Lord and keep seeking Him, and more importantly, stay in His presence, He has great things in store for you to prosper you. Just keep trusting, things will work out in the end. As time passed, I ended up meeting my soul mate, who was from Addington.

Meeting my soul mate

I was 18 years old at the time, working in the catering industry. After work, I agreed to meet my friend for a drink at our regular wine bar. A new hip spot to be seen in, it was a busy place with loud music, like hip hop, soul and reggae, which I loved.

Just before I left work, I had a call from my friend saying he couldn't meet up, but I still went ahead to the bar. I had a couple of drinks and was thinking of heading home and calling it a day, when
five girls walked in and sat next to where I was. I recognised one of them from school and started chatting, catching up on old times. They said they were going to the club next door and invited me to come along. I was finishing my drink when another lovely lady walked in. One of their friends, Nikki. I found out later that Nikki was waiting outside for 20 minutes, not realising her friends were already inside.

 I still remember it all clearly in my mind. She wore blue jeans, a matching outfit, with a long gold chain. As she walked in, it was like time slowed down for me. She looked gorgeous. We spoke briefly, then they invited me to join them in going to the club next door to the office. I had just enough money to get into the club. I was down to my last £5, and that went a lot further in them days. An example was that on a Saturday, I could get a return journey on the bus from home, get McDonald's, and still have change left from £4, amazing.
So, we all went to the club, which was playing classic, soul and R&B. I started to get my groove on, then took a break from the dance floor and noticed that Nikki, for a moment, was separated from her friends. She was just standing there enjoying the music. So, we started talking from the start. We made a connection and got on well, like two pieces of a jigsaw

puzzle coming together. We could have stayed there all night just talking, it was like two spirits coming together, I can't explain it. Even though I did not know the Lord at the time, I still believe angels were involved. The Lord can instruct them to prepare a place or a person for you. What amazing love the Lord has for us, that even when I was in sin, He still considered me.

We got on well, then decided to leave the club. I walked Nikki down to the taxi station; it was like time had slowed down. What a blessing, just goes to show you the best things in life sometimes happen when you least expect it. Guaranteed that if I went out that night with the intention of meeting someone, it would not have happened. So, whatever you want in life, don't stress and apply too much unnecessary pressure, just have faith and put the matter in the hands of the Lord. Chill, enjoy your day, and then the answer will find you. So, we said our goodbyes and agreed to meet up the next day, and the rest is history. We spent most of our spare time together. Nikki passed her driving test before me, so we would drive for miles just enjoying each other's company and hanging out. We usually ended up by the seaside and loved watching the waves early morning, coming in and out, and the amazing sunsets. The Bible said those who find a wife find a good thing. I felt in my heart she was my soul mate.

In time, we bought our first flat, and after a few years together, I then took Nikki out for a romantic meal, got down on one knee, and proposed. I dropped the big question, "Will you marry me?"
She, of course, said 'yes', so we got married. What a great day that was! I remember waking up that morning thinking I was getting married. My best man, my friends and I had to go and pick up our suits in Croydon. It was a typically busy Saturday morning, and we got lots of attention walking down High Street wearing our tuxedos. I remember a lady bus driver shouting, "Very nice lads."

So, on the day, with anticipation, I was waiting for the wedding car to arrive. It emerged with Nikki's face smiling inside, looking beautiful like an angel. She emerged from the wedding car, a Mercedes, and my best man kept making me laugh, but kept me calm at the same time.

The weather in the morning was cloudy, but by midday, when we came out for pictures, it had brightened up really well. It was a nice sunny day for the pictures in the garden. The only thing was that Nikki's only sister was not able to attend because she was ill in the hospital. I felt really bad that she could not make it!

So, we did the unthinkable and took the wedding to her in the hospital. We had our chauffeur drop us off at the hospital after the wedding. Nikki, my best man, my in-laws and I walked down the aisle of the hospital with all the nurses and staff clapping their hands. We spent about an hour there before moving on to the reception. Even my brother and his wife from America came over to our wedding. I asked him to be the Master of Ceremonies at the reception. It was full of family, friends, and even friends from work turned up. It was an open bar evening, with plenty of Jamaican food and an English buffet. Everyone was coming up to us, wishing the best for the future. The DJ was excellent, it had a really nice atmosphere. When we got home that night, we were so tired, we had so many presents to open, and cards wishing the best filled the whole room. In the morning, we jetted off to Africa for our honeymoon. It was great, and here, twenty years later, we are still together, bless the Lord.

Here are a few keys to a good marriage relationship:
- **Honour**
  Honouring each other is the most important I think. Even in the Bible, in the Ten Commandments, the first five commandments deal with the word 'honour'. Learn what this is – it's respect for each other.

Always talk highly about each other in front of people, and have a strong defence when needed. In your actions, it should be apparent how much you love each other on a daily basis.

- **Communication**
It's very important to be able to speak to each other, whatever's on your mind, good or bad. The problem is when you don't voice your concerns and let them build up throughout the day, until the next day. It will just get worse and harder to resolve.

"Be ye angry, and sin not. Let not the sun go down upon your wrath."
Ephesians 4:26 (KJV)

So, the Lord is saying, before you go to bed, if you are angry, make things right. Address the matter whether financial problems, commitments, sex, emotional lack, appreciation for each other, selfishness, trust or anger.

- **Truth**
Always be open and honest, with nothing hidden.
- **Work**
Be prepared to work at it, nothing in life just happens without work. We all were designed to work, even the Lord Jesus Himself had to work for a living before He started His ministry as a carpenter. You have to work at marriage to make it work.

My Salvation

If given the opportunity to spend time in the presence of a great person like royalty, there are protocols to follow. You just won't be able to get full access straight away, and that's the desire of many to be in the presence of greatness, to have a new, reformed life. If not just for the experience, but before I pressed into great things in the future. In this chapter, things continued in my life and got from bad to worse with things at home and work. It seemed like I was under attack from all sides, just problems everywhere, and relationships. Like an example with my wife, I never knew how to open up my heart and show my true feelings, how I felt, and I even found it hard to say I love you to my partner. I was like a macho guy with too much pride. I believe there are many guys in this position. They don't know how to open up and share their heart with the one they love. It's one of the biggest reasons for divorce in the world, like a lack of communication. After I came to salvation with Jesus, His love showed me how to open up and share my heart with effective communication with Nikki and everyone around me.

Anyway, everything felt like it was closing in on me, and there was no way out. I just remember being and feeling so alone and fed up all the time, even though I was in a relationship, and most of the time, had people around me and a good social life. I was used to having a large family around me, but I was still alone. I think this may be the case for a lot of people out there, you just feel alone and unloved, and that no one cares. Just remember Jesus loves you, and He's there for you always, just give Him a call.

"Verily, verily, I say unto you, Except a corn of wheat fall unto the ground and die, it abideth alone: but if it die, it bringeth forth much fruit."
John 12:24 (KJV)

To understand this statement, in farming or gardening, the seed, which contains the fullest potential of life, ceases to be a seed when it dies, so that the plant inside may live. Essentially, its original form has died, and the seed becomes something new. So, this resembles our lives, and walking with the Lord, it's a process of dying, until you get to a point when the flesh can no longer produce, letting the spirit take over. The Lord gives you a new name and identity, like Abram, then He changed his name to Abraham when he reached perfection.

"Neither shall thy name any more be called Abram, but thy name shall be Abraham; For a father of many nations have I made thee."
Genesis 17:5 (KJV)

This also shows me that a life without God is being *alone* in this world, learning to die to our selfish needs, and the works of the flesh, and trusting God, and much fruit will come.

In June 1987, I was invited by a friend to come along to New Life Christian centre, an evening service at a local fellowship, so my friend and I turned up and sat right at the back of the congregation, talking and messing around.

The preacher that evening was a young, ordinary-looking guy, wearing jeans and a t-shirt. His message was even more ordinary: *"What do you secure your life on?"* He said many people secure their life on different things, like material things, having a nice car, having music in their life, having a nice sound system and having a nice house. He continued saying many people secure their life on having a beautiful wife, family, kids, having close friends, having a good job with authority, a high level of education, a doctor's or master's degree, or motorsport. With some people, the case is being a member at their local pub, or an organisation where you look forward to having a beer or a glass of wine at the end of the day. He continued saying many people secure their life by taking drugs, where it's constantly looking forward to the next fix. It's just a temporary answer to problems in your life. He then said, "Come to Jesus, He will fix you on a natural high and have I mentioned it's a free gift to you today, so receive it."

With all these things just mentioned, it's not that the Lord is against these things because Jesus commands us to love one another like our friends and family, and even strangers. It's nice to have nice things like cars and houses. The danger is what we put *first* in our lives, what takes priority over everything else. *This is when you secure your life on it,* then these things become your God without you realising it.

"But seek ye first the kingdom of God, and his righteousness; and all these things shall be added unto you."
Matthew 6:33 (KJV)

Another big one, the preacher continued talking about, was *money,* where the goal is to earn as much as possible to find happiness. It's scriptural to work, the Bible says if a man does not work, he should not eat.

"No man can serve two masters: for either he will hate the one, and love the other; or else he will hold to the one, and despise the other. Ye cannot serve God and mammon."
Matthew 6:24 (KJV)

"For the love of money is the root of all evil: which while some coveted after, they have erred from the faith, and pierced themselves through with many sorrows."
1 Timothy 6:10 (KJV)

As the preacher continued, his words felt like not ordinary words but words with substance and power. It started to cut right through me, like a sword.

"And take the helmet of salvation, and the sword of the Spirit, which is the word of God."
Ephesians 6:17 (KJV)

He carried on saying that many people secure their life by having a certain lifestyle they are accustomed to, and in a comfort zone. So, they felt like they did not need God, but that's simply because they never experienced God!

"Because thou sayest, I am rich and increased with goods, and have need of nothing,and knowest not that you are wretched, and miserable, and poorand blind and naked."
Revelations 3:17 (KJV)

This described my life, I was wretched and miserable.

As the preacher continued, I was trying to hold back the tears flowing. I was still trying to look cool in front of my friend, but I could not hold back the tears any longer. It just came forth like a mighty river flowing down my face. That night, it felt like a weight had lifted off me, it felt like what he was saying was addressed to me, and that I was the only one in the room, even though over a thousand were there.

The Bible says the Holy Spirit is a witness to God's word. At the time, it was like the spirit was there with me, confirming God's word; it was an amazing experience. After the service was over, on the way home, I could not stop thinking about what had just happened. I looked down at my hands, and I was shaking from the experience. The strange thing it was not a cold evening, so it was not the weather. It must have been the power of God and the effects of the Word spoken to me. The next day, a Sunday morning, I still had this clearly in my mind: "What do you secure your life on?" This was because I knew that what I was securing my life on was material things, which I gave priority in my life.

It got to Monday morning, and I was still thinking about what the preacher said. At the time, I had sold my car and was temporarily on my push bike going to work. I got to work, still thinking about what the preacher said. I could not get it out of my mind, "What do you secure your life on?" The only way to describe it is like an angel repeating this, saying to me, over and over again.

The amazing presence of God

The Monday evening, I came home from work, very tired after riding home on my pushbike, but still thinking about what the preacher said. I went to my room and prayed *my first real prayer* to the Lord Jesus. I kneeled down and said, "Lord, I give you thanks for today and that wonderful message I heard on sat evening. Lord Jesus, help me to let go of 'What I'm securing my life on' and help me to learn to put you first in everything I do in my life."

As I said this, my room felt like it started to shake like an earthquake, and I was being transported somewhere else. With tears flowing down my face, I started to shake violently. I thought to myself, "What's going on here?" I knew I was entering *God's amazing presence*. I made a commitment to the Lord, I said, "I will serve you, Lord, no matter what life throws at me, even if I end up staying on my push bike for the rest of my life, I will serve you, Lord." Then the Lord took me in a vision: I was out hiking one day in the countryside and came near the edge and slipped and fell off a high mountain cliff, managing to cling to a rocky side a little way down. I desperately needed rescuing, I was holding tight to a rock in case I fell. I then tried to reach for my phone to call for help.

All of a sudden, this bright light appeared above me. As the light got closer and brighter, it looked like a shining light through the figure of a man. It was Jesus, then He spoke to me and said, *"Let go and reach up to my hand."* I had to let go of the rock with one hand to reach Him. I said, "I don't know if I can, Lord." I believe the Lord was also speaking within my spirit, about me letting go of my past life to reach up to touch Him for a new life. I believe the rock represented my old life, a hard place of sin, with no hope, and everything that I was securing it on.

Then He said to me a second time, *"Let go and reach up to my hand."* I then looked down at my other hand, and *I was astonished to see that this dark, evil creature from hell was holding me back with its claws gripping my other hand, preventing me from letting go.* Then Jesus said for the third time, *"Let go and reach up to my hand."* This evil creature was still holding me back. I was trying my best to shake it off, then with all my strength and real determination, I said, *"In the name of Jesus, let me go satan."* As I said this, it was like the chains broke off me and I was free, for the first time in my life.

Praise God! I then reached out my hand to Jesus to lift me up. As He touched me, it felt like fire going through my body, and the heat of His touch was soothing to my soul. His eyes were calming, like many oceans. As He took both my hands and lifted me clear of the mounting, it was at that moment that I felt His love and compassion and His peace like nothing else in this world. All this hit me at once with one touch of His hands, an amazing experience.

After this, the Lord spoke to my spirit and confirmed that it was salvation, and I just entered into a new life with Him. "The evil creature was fighting you because where I'm taking you, it's going to *cause major damage to his kingdom of darkness.*"

At this time, I was still on my bedroom floor, crying and thanking God for giving me victory over the evil one. His presence filled the whole room like a cloud, I was experiencing time *in God's amazing presence* for the first time. Then I saw 2 Samuel 23:2 –

"The Spirit of the LORD spake by me, and his word was in my tongue." (KJV)

The Lord was trying to show me that His word spoken in His presence can be like fire. So, I started reading His word, the Bible, and this continued for over five hours. It realistically felt like one hour had passed. Just spending time in His presence, there was a shift and transition from Greenwich, mean time to heaven's domain where there's 'no time'. I felt real peace because Jesus is the Prince of Peace.

"As for God, his way is perfect; the Word of the Lord is tried: he is a buckler to all them that trust in Him."
2 Samuel 22:31 (KJV)

As I carried on reading the Bible, it just started to come *alive* to me. It was like actually being there when it happened, like watching a movie, then being placed in a live chapter of filming it, making it come alive!!! Amen. I started experiencing the revelation of His word.

"That which is born of the flesh is flesh; and that which is born of the spirit is spirit."
John 3:6-7 (KJV)

Marvel not that I said unto you; you must be born again. So, this was a transforming time for me as I was born again there on my bedroom floor. You're so amazing, Lord.

"Being born again, not of corruptible seed, but of incorruptible, by the Word of God, which liveth and abideth for ever."
1 Peter 1:23 (KJV)

So, I eventually went to sleep that night. I woke up the next morning, and it felt like a new world. Looking out the window, the sun seemed brighter, flowers a lot more vibrant, and everything just had a glow to it. It's like coming from nothing to everything. What a great feeling. It felt like heaven, and angels were rejoicing with me. The next day at work, I remember thinking I could not wait to get back to God's amazing presence.

"Likewise, I say unto you, there is joy in the presence of angels of God over one sinner that repenteth."
Luke 15:10 (KJV)

From a young age, I had a seed to worship the Lord sown in my life, but we still have a free will to choose light or darkness, heaven or hell. The thing is, Satan does not come in His natural form.

"And no marvel; for Satan himself is transformed into an angel of light."
2 Corinthians 11:14 (KJV)

He will do anything to transform himself to entice you from the gospel. You just have to be strong and determined to win. The Word says we are more than conquerors, also it says resist the devil and he will flee. The Bible says greater is He that is within, than he in the world, so the light in us is stronger than darkness, if we activate our faith.

So, my first day after coming to the Lord was so amazing. In His amazing presence was such peace I felt inside me. It was around the same time that the UK experienced the first Christian channel, God TV. It first only came on for four hours a day, starting at 4 am. I was completely glued to watching it, and I used to set my alarm clock so I would never miss a program. My spirit was drawn every morning like a thirsty man in a hot desert. This was like a magnet that drew me into the wonderful presence of the Lord. It then made me think who was the first person in the Bible to experience the presence of God, and how they lost it.

So, I started from the beginning in the book Genesis, from day one, Adam and Eve were the first. In the Garden of Eden, they lived in God's presence. The Bible says Adam walked with the Lord. He was in constant union with God, talking to Him, God speaking back to him and having fellowship together. In a close, intimate relationship where only God is exalted above everything on earth. It's this relationship that God originally intended for us to have with Him, where we can open up our hearts to Him and enter the deep places of God. We can explore the true love of God, which passes all understanding and His amazing presence, which covers us.

"And God said, Let us make man in our image, after our likeness: and let them have dominion over the fish of the sea, and over the fowl of the air, and over the cattle, and over all the earth, and over every creeping thing that creepeth upon the earth."
Genesis 1:26 (KJV)

Let's break this down a little. "Let us make man in our image" - the word 'us' means more than one, that's why in the New Testament Jesus said, "If you have seen me, you have also seen the Father God." In the beginning, the spirit of God moved upon the face of the waters. It's like the spirit was already in position, moving and ready to receive instruction from the Word, which is Jesus.
"And the Word was made flesh, and dwelt among us."
John 1:14 (KJV)

When Jesus transformed into a man, how glorious that the Almighty, the creator of heaven and earth, laid down His Glory and majesty and power, and took on human flesh because of His love for us. It changed our destiny and released us from captivity. What amazing love!

Back to Genesis 1, so after the Holy Spirit received the Word and God gave the command, there we have the Holy Trinity working in unity together. God said, "Let us make man in our image." If I take a picture of something, I get an image. It's like looking in the mirror, you get a reflection. What good news! This means we are made in the likeness of God. We are in His image, it does not stop there and continues saying, we are also in His

Likeness, which means having the characteristics of someone, or resemblance. This is amazing. We are more like God than we think.

What's my character like? Sometimes I get sad or happy in life's ups and downs. There are decisions to say 'yes' or 'no'. The choice to choose good or evil. God is like that, but the Bible says God is a good God, a wonderful counsellor, a Prince of Peace. His love for us goes beyond our *understanding* or *comprehension*. It reaches the Heavens and it's deeper than the ocean. His love is like a consuming fire breaking through every barrier. No matter what your history, His love covers all sin, and there's hope for everybody.

So, the Lord said, "Let mankind have dominion." The word means the power or right of governing and controlling sovereign authority, rule, and territory of a ruler, absolute ownership. So, when Adam gave names to all the animals, this was power. He had control and authority. So, when the devil came in the form of a serpent, he was more subtle and craftier than any other living creature of the fields that the Lord God had made. He came first to strip Adam and Eve of their dominion, their control and power and authority, and most of all their walk with God. His sole purpose is to steal, kill and destroy. Man had constant contact with heaven because Adam *walked with the Lord in the garden*, in perfect unity with the Father, Son, and Holy Spirit.

Adam was pure and uncorrupted. He was sinless and holy and sanctified, most of all the presence of God was present all in His Glory. Without measure, in a place of more than enough. No lack, and no seasons like winter, summer, autumn and spring. Adam was free to enjoy the constant good weather consistently. Where the *presence of the Lord is, there is only one season*. The glory and abundance were in the trees in Eden, and the garden bore constant fruit with the waters coming from underground because the Lord had not sent the rain yet. Daily, we need to be in the presence of God continually, connected to the underground source of God's blessings for our lives.

In Eden, God also placed a wall of protection around the garden.

"Cherubims, and a flaming sword which turned every way, to keep the way of the tree of life."
Genesis 3:24(KJV)

Adam and Eve were free from any curses like sin and death. They had glorified bodies, the same bodies the second Adam, Jesus, came back with, to redeem what was lost in the resurrection. What an amazing thought! When we meet the Lord in glory, we will get the same body. Adam was free from death. Yes, designed to live forever in eternity. No sickness, no stress. He was made *perfect, with no flaws*. His mind was complete and extremely intelligent, knowledgeable, and with great wisdom and memory.

"Now the Lord had formed out of the ground all the wild animals and all the birds in the sky. He brought them to the man to see what he would name them; and whatever the man called each living creature, that was its name."
Genesis 2:19 (NIV)

So, the man gave names to all livestock, the birds in the sky, and wild animals. Just the birds alone are over 11,000 different species in the world. The different types of animals have 1.5 million species and 8.7 million different living animals. Wow! Adam named every single one of them. What a great, amazing memory.

His memory started to diminish when sin was introduced to the scene, when Adam and Eve chose to disobey the instructions given not to eat from the Tree of Knowledge of Good and Evil. This commandment was more for their protection, from sin and death.

"And when the woman saw that the tree was good for food, and that it was pleasant to the eyes, and a tree to be desired to make one wise, she took of the fruit thereof, and did eat, and gave also unto her husband with her, and he did eat."
Genesis 3:6 (KJV)

Then the Word says they heard the voice of the Lord God walking in the garden, and Adam and Eve hid themselves from the presence of God. The Lord called unto Adam, "Where are you?" Adam said, "I heard thy voice, but I was afraid, because I was naked and hid myself," he said, "Who told you that you were naked? Hast thou eaten from the tree, whereof I commanded you not to eat?"

Then Adam said, "The woman you gave me, she gave me of the tree and I did eat."
They were separated from God's presence. All of a sudden, Adam and Eve were in the flesh. The Holy Spirit of God departed. Looking at themselves, they felt naked, alone, vulnerable, weak and lost their authority and power which they had. They were ashamed the same way we are with our sins and shortcomings in life, and fearful of the future without Christ in our lives.

The word 'afraid' was the first thing Adam said to the Lord. The Lord asked Adam if he had eaten from the Tree of Life, and his excuse was he said the woman, whom the Lord had given to him, ate from the tree first and then gave it to him. Still, no confession was given from Adam to the Lord. When we pass the buck with excuses in our lives and when it comes to knowing Christ, like Eve replied, "The serpent tricked me then I ate from the tree."

This is where it all started, making excuses to God, with no confession for our sins, and the way we live our lives. You can have a rich man say, "I don't need God as I have everything I need in my life," passing the buck with excuses, or it could be a poor man saying, "If God exists, get me off the street." No more excuses given; the Lord wants to meet with you wherever you are. No matter what situation you are in, you could be a famous person who has worked hard all their life, with a good career, a beautiful family and a luxurious home, more than any man could want. I ask you to stop for a second and check how you feel deep inside your heart. If you feel lonely, sad or fearful, you need Jesus in your life. If a scientist created a robot and programmed it to do different things, but the heart of the robot was a microchip, if it were removed or missing, the robot would malfunction. As this is missing something vital to operate to its full potential, the same is true in our lives without the presence of God. We are also missing something vital in our lives to operate, and we are malfunctioning. You could be a minister sharing the gospel, but without the presence of God and the Holy Spirit, it's just the flesh, and you will simply wear yourself out. The Lord does not take pleasure in the flesh; He resides in the spirit.

So, judgment came to the devil first, the tempter, the evil one. I believe at this stage he was laughing at the woman for yielding to his temptation, laughing his head off, thinking he had won the fight. Then God gave the devil a picture of his future in his laughter and said, *"The same woman you have deceived her seed will come back and crush your head."*

"And I will put enmity between thee and the woman, and between thy seed, and her seed, it shall BRUISE THY HEAD, AND THOU SHALT BRUISE HIS HEEL."
Genesis 3:15 (KJV)
This tells me that *God was talking about over two thousand years in the future*, when Mary, a virgin, was with a child. So, it started with signs in the heavens, the wise men had studied astrology for a long time, and they

followed the prophecy of the star of Bethlehem. When angel Gabriel was sent to the virgin Mary, and said, "You are highly favored, the Lord is with you, bless you among women, the Holy Spirit shall come upon you and the power of the highest shall overshadow you therefore the holy thing that shall be born of thee shall be called the son of God."

The only people nearby to tell the good news to were the shepherds as they watched their sheep by night. The angel of the Lord came upon them and the glory of the Lord shone over them. The angel said unto them, *"Today, for onto you is born today in the city of David, a saviour which is Christ the Lord."*

When a child is in their mother's womb, you can trace the DNA and find who the father is. Mary was still a virgin, so the blood type came from heaven. I thought why did God have to send His son through Mary? Why not send Jesus as a spirit to earth in His natural form? Then the answer came to me. God is sovereign as His word, I believe God will never violate His word, and God is limited by His word.

"And God said, Let us make man in our image, after our likeness and LET THEM HAVE DOMINION over the fish of the sea, and over the fowl of the air, and over the cattle, and over all the earth, and over every creeping thing that creepeth upon the earth."
Genesis 1:26 (KJV)

In this scripture, God is talking about the spirit and body of mankind to rule on earth, so God was limited by His word. He could not come in His natural form, He had to come through a woman, which makes His body and spirit like a legal being on earth.
The punishment for the woman and man was in Genesis 3:16-19 –

"Unto the woman he said, I will greatly multiply thy sorrow and thy conception; in sorrow thou shalt bring forth children; and thy desire shall be to thy husband, and he shall rule over thee." (KJV)

"And unto Adam he said, Because thou hast hearkened unto the voice of thy wife, and hast eaten of the tree, of which I commanded thee, saying, thou shalt not eat of it: cursed is the ground for thy sake; in sorrow shalt thou eat of it all the days of thy life;" (KJV)

So, death is pronounced to us through our earthly bodies through the sin of the first Adam.

Jesus is also known as the second Adam because over 2,000 years ago he came to reverse the curse of sin and death. *Jesus paid the price for us to enter back into time in God's presence.*
"By which also he went and preached unto the spirits in prison;"
1 Peter 3:19 (KJV)

Because He died, He went into the underworld, hell itself, for three days and was face to face with the devil, and spoiled principalities and powers. Jesus, the perfect man, sinless, then took the keys of death and hell from the devil, preached to the saints and then God raised Him victoriously from the dead. How amazing is that!

"I am he that liveth, and was dead; and behold, I am alive for evermore, Amen; and have the keys of hell and of death."
Revelation 1:18 (KJV)

So, giving us full access to His holy presence, which was lost from Adam and Eve! I believe when God said, "Thou shalt surely die," to Adam, He meant it in more ways than one. Firstly, He meant it as for our mortal bodies, all will all see death and the grave one day, unless caught up to meet Him on His second return to earth. Secondly, God spoke about spiritual death, *which is being severed from the presence of God*. Before man sinned, the plan of God was for us to live forever, in that body. Because of sin and corruption, it enslaved us to the law of sin and death. We can, through salvation, choose where our spirit/soul goes, either heaven or hell. The main thing now is that through Jesus, we have been given full *access* to the presence of God, so let's all enter in.

Moses also spent a lot of time in the presence of God. His first experience was at 80 years old. When he saw a burning bush in the distance and the leaves were not consumed, he turned to see this great sight. He could have walked away and carried on his business, but from day one, Moses had a deep desire to experience the presence of God. As he came into it, God spoke to him, to come no closer. "Take off your shoes because you're standing on holy ground," God said the same thing to the priest, in the future, regarding the Tabernacle. The significance of this is to remind man that, because of the law, sin and death ruled the human body at that time.

So, Moses was restricted to not coming any closer, or he would die. The glory of God is so pure, sin could not come any further, and casting off His shoes symbolised restoration and reinstatement of status. In the ancient world, slaves often went barefoot, while free men wore shoes, so man lost His status because of sin. Jesus had not yet been offered up as a sacrifice to break the curse of sin and death, but Moses was the only one in the Bible who in God's presence, chose to speak to him face to face.

"And the LORD spake unto Moses face to face, as a man speaketh unto his friend. And he turned again into the camp: but his servant Joshua, the son of Nun, a young man, departed not out of the tabernacle. And Moses said unto the LORD, See, thou sayest unto me, Bring up this people: and thou hast not let me know whom thou wilt send with me. Yet thou hast said, I know thee by name, and thou hast also found grace in my sight. Now

therefore, I pray thee if I have found grace in thy sight, shew me now thy way, that I may know thee, that I may find grace in thy sight: and consider that this nation is thy people. And he said, My presence shall go with thee, and I will give thee rest. And he said unto him, If thy presence go not with me, carry us not up hence."
Exodus 33:11-15 (KJV)

You see, Moses discovered what it is to be in the Lord's presence, that's why he said, "I will not go from this place without your presence." I love this bit where Joshua stayed in the presence of God, because it's so *sweet and energising, like a magnet pulling you back in.* You just want more and more. He did not want to come out of it. Because we've simply been designed in the original blueprint for mankind to be in His wonderful presence 24/7, and that is why when we are in the glory of God, our spirit is at home. It just wants to remain there, it's so amazing. We need the presence of God in our Christian Walk more than anything, and to have real determination like Moses.

So, *STOP what you're doing today and say, "I will not live another day without your presence."* I believe once you've experienced and tasted something like the presence of God, nothing else comes close to it in this world, until we see God in heaven. Without His presence, everything is empty, meaningless and pointless. Someone could be the best preacher in the world, but without the Lord's presence, it's just words with no power, just the flesh in action! To affect people, you need the spirit mixed with the Word to have a lasting changed life. The book of Acts is a true example of the power and effectiveness of the presence of God. On the Day of Pentecost, the Holy Spirit fell on the disciples, and the power of God was released. Over 3,000 people got saved, and their lives were transformed; it was a divine shift in the multiplication of souls.
And that's how many people still live their lives today, even some religious groups that go by a set of rules, 'do's and don't's', but still without God's

presence, even though we may do many works in His name and good deeds.

"Knowing that a man is not justified by works of the law, but by the faith of Jesus Christ, even we have believed in Jesus Christ, that we might be justified by faith of Christ."
Galatians 2:16 (KJV)

I believe we can do many things for God, but *without His presence, nothing means anything.*

"Many will say to me in that day, 'Lord, Lord, have we not prophesied in thy name? and in thy name have cast out devils? and in thy name done many wonderful works?
And then will I profess unto them, I never knew you; depart from me, ye that work iniquity."
Matthew 7:22-23 (KJV)

Here is another great example glory and power of God.

"And Moses went up into the mount, and a cloud covered the mount. And the glory of the LORD abode upon mount Sinai, and the cloud covered it six days: and the seventh day he called unto Moses out of the midst of the cloud. And the sight of the glory of the LORD was like devouring fire on the top of the mount in the eyes of the children of Israel. And Moses went into the midst of the cloud, and gat him up into the mount: and Moses was in the mount forty days and forty nights."
Exodus 24:15-18 (KJV)

I think this is so amazing. There are two things: first thing - the cloud covered it for six days, then on the seventh day the Lord called Moses. I always thought to myself, "What were they doing up there for six days to pass the time?" Before the Lord spoke to him, I believe God's presence was so strong, the Lord did not need to speak. The Bible says that when we do not know what to pray, the Holy Spirit will make intercession for us. So, I believe the Holy Spirit, before God spoke, was interceding with words that were spoken.

Then Moses went into the midst of the cloud and was there for *forty days and nights*. It just blows my mind how he could spend forty days and nights in one place without getting bored. You think in those days there was no Sky TV, no PlayStation, no social media, no internet, just the presence of God, which is all we need; He fulfils, all in all.

Before my experience with God, I could not understand this; now I do! When you enter God's amazing presence, there's a transition in time. From earthly time to heavenly time, just like on the Mount of Transfiguration. Heaven came to where they were.

"And after six days, Jesus taketh Peter, James, and John his brother, and bringeth them up into an high mountain apart, and was transfigured before them: and his face did shine as the sun, and his raiment was white as the light. And behold, there appeared unto them Moses and Elias talking with him. Then answered Peter, and said unto Jesus, Lord, it is good for us to be here: if thou wilt; let us make here three tabernacles; one for thee, and one for Moses, and one for Elias. While he spake, behold, a bright cloud overshadowed them; and behold a voice out of the cloud, which said, This is my beloved son, in whom I am well pleased; hear ye him."
Matthew 17:1-5 (KJV)

You see, in the presence of God, you take on a new *form* because the Word says Jesus was transfigured, in other words, He took on His heavenly form.

"But beloved, be not ignorant of this one thing, that one day is with the Lord as a thousand years, and a thousand years as one day."
2 Peter 3:8 (KJV)

What I understand is that heaven's time is not the same as Earth's time; that's why Moses was able to spend forty days in His presence. The glory of God must have felt like one day. The same thing happened to me many times while on my knees praying, looking at the time, thinking that only one hour had passed, when in fact, six hours had passed. Praise God.

In the presence of God, as you take on a new form, you discover who you really are in Christ. Just like Saul on the road to Damascus.

"And as he journeyed, he came near Damascus: and suddenly there shined round about him a light from heaven: and he fell to the earth, and heard a voice saying unto Him, Saul, Saul, why persecutest thou me?"
Acts 9:3-4 (KJV)

Then Saul said, "What will you have me to do, Lord?" It was in this that Saul discovered who he really was in Christ and the purpose of his life. There have been many instances in the Word, where the Lord has transformed people in His presence, given them a new identity and a name change like Abram.

"And when Abram was nightly nine years old, the LORD appeared to Abram, and said unto him, I am the Almighty God; walk before me and be thou perfect."
Genesis 17:1(KJV)
And:
"Neither shall thy name any more be called Abram, but thy name shall be Abraham; for a father of many nations have I made thee."
Genesis 17:5 (KJV)

You see, the whole process in Abraham's life continued till the Lord perfected His work in him. I have also noticed that when you're in God's presence, it makes you hungry for more of Him. Just like Moses was in the glory on the Mount when he said to the Lord, "If I may see your face, Lord." Then the Lord said, "No one can see my face and live, but I will put you in the cliffs of the rock and pass by you and you see my back part of my glory." I think it's amazing, it's good to be hungry and thirsty for more of God, just never be satisfied. With what you have got, there's always more.

"For I will pour water upon him that is thirsty, and floods upon the dry ground."
Isaiah 44:3 (KJV)

So, in the dry places in our lives, we let Jesus come in and give us a true life worth living. We need to enter the presence of God and let the glory of the Lord fill the place where we are. I pray for you now in the name of Jesus that as you read this book, you will be transformed in the fullness of His presence, and I rebuke Satan and the whole of hell in your life and any hindrances, holding you back from where you need to be, in Jesus' name, amen.

How to enter God's presence

The first thing you need is to be born again into the family of God. In a quiet time to yourself, you make an open confession to the Lord. *Romans 10:9 says that if thou shalt confess with thy mouth the Lord Jesus, and shalt believe in thine heart that God hath raised Him from the dead, thou shalt be saved.* After saying this with all your heart, and acknowledging Jesus died to save you from your sins, you shall be saved.

"For God so loved the world, that he gave his only begotten son, that whosoever believeth in him should not perish, but have everlasting life." John 3:16 (KJV)

Welcome now to the Kingdom of God, all of heaven and the holy angels are celebrating your 'coming out' from a life of sin and darkness into His glorious light. You are now justified from the things to come, and you are now freed from the law of sin and death, glory to God, amen and amen.

As you enter into God's presence in your daily prayer time, there is much opposition in the spirit. The thing is, the enemy does not want you to enter into the Lord's presence, because if you do, it is like you having the keys to bring down his kingdom, with the power of God. So, he will send a Spirit of distraction your way to distract you from entering God's presence. It seems from the moment you kneel down to pray, something comes to distract you, like the phone might ring with friends asking you to come out. Out of nowhere someone turns up to visit you, your family might need you for something, or the dog might start barking, requesting a walk, and the list goes on and on.

As you start to pray, your mind will start to wander to things not pertaining to the Word of God. Like, shall I go and watch a movie, go and listen to some music, or go and watch a football match, whatever you enjoy doing, etc. You see, the flesh, the carnal side of man, is still alive and fighting. You see, when this happens, there's no power yet, because Jesus resides in the spirit, not the flesh. The flesh is already cursed from when Adam and Eve first sinned, and the Lord passed judgment that their flesh, their body, will now go back to the ground from which it came.

That's why when Jesus was at the well with the woman of Samaria.

"...but the hour cometh, and now is, when the true worshipers shall worship the Father in spirit and in truth: for the Father seeketh such to worship him."
John 4:23 (KJV)
I like that portion, The Father is on the hunt for true worshipers!! and we are daily hunting to find His presence.

What a thing when we can be truly open our hearts in *truth* to God in seeking Him. It's like there's a battle going on between the flesh verses the spirit. Paul, in the New Testament, says the following:

"And they that are Christ's have crucified the flesh with the affections and lust."
Galatians 5:24 (KJV)
We must crucify the flesh to walk in the spirit. This is not easy, or instant. It's a real battle, but we have been assured victory through Christ, and as an example, Jesus Himself had to battle with the flesh, the carnal side of His body, versus His spirit, in the Garden of Gethsemane leading up to the Crucifixion. You have to remember that Jesus was part man and part God. It is why He understands all our pain and stresses and everything we could possibly go through in our lives.

"And he took with him Peter and the two sons of Zebedee, and began to be sorrowful and very heavy. Then saith he unto them, my soul is exceeding sorrowful, even unto death: tarry ye here, and watch with me. And He went a little further and fell on his face, and prayed saying, O my Father, if it be possible, let this cup pass from me: nevertheless not as I will, but as thou wilt." (KJV)
Matthew 26:37-39

Then, Jesus continued to seek company because the carnal side of Him needed the social company of people, someone to speak to, and in a desperate time of need, to share a burden with His disciples. The flesh was still alive, and the battle was still continuing. At this point, a lot of us would just give up, or go and watch a movie or something. The thing is, before we get a real breakthrough in the spirit, we must remember that there is a war raging and much evil opposing us, to reach the goal, hoping that you will give up early.

"He went away again the second time, and prayed saying, O my Father, if this cup may not pass away from me, except I drink it, thy will be done.' And he came and found them asleep again. For their eyes were heavy."
Matthew 26:42-43

At this stage in prayer, there is still no breakthrough, the battle is still raging, the flesh is still winning, and the demons behind it are throwing all their arsenal at you. At this stage, desperately hoping that you will quit and give up. So be encouraged today and remember that when the heat is turned up in the battlefield, and being attacked on every side, it means you're very close to breakthrough and victory. Just hold your ground, keep standing even though your body is screaming otherwise in the way you feel, if you feel fed up, discouraged, stressed, etc. These are all feelings from the flesh, declaring you're not there yet. Just keep pushing on with the strength you have left.

"And he left them, and went away again, and prayed the third time, saying the same words."
Matthew 26:44 (KJV)

It was then that Jesus got the breakthrough from the carnal flesh to the spirit. *Victory,* then all power was released from the Father in heaven to complete the task of Calvary. Before, Jesus was saying, "Let this cup pass by me," but now His speech had changed. He was in a new place, the amazing presence of God, and He started speaking from the spirit not the flesh. The carnal just lost the battle, thy will be done. He was ready now to do the work. The victory over Satan was won right there before Jesus went to the cross, in the garden in the early hours of the morning, praise God.

So, the first key to entering His presence is determination. You need lots, because Jesus had lots of determination to reach a goal. Be willing to stay there until you get the breakthrough, like *Thomas Edison,* the famous inventor of the incandescent light bulb. He had a strong determination to succeed. I think to myself, this is the determination we need to enter time in God's presence and to reach goals in life.

"I press toward the mark for the prize of the high calling of God in Christ Jesus."
Philippians 3:14 (KJV)

Paul is saying we are pressing towards the mark. We must remember in our daily prayer time, *there's a MARK to reach.*

The second key to entering God's presence is the spirit breaking through the carnal flesh, to that holy place in Christ Jesus. It's a similar case when an aircraft approaches the mark of the sound barrier, also known as the sonic barrier of 767 mph. It undergoes an abruptly increasing drag force induced by compression of the surrounding air when travelling near the speed of sound.

Explanation: *There is no physical barrier at the speed of sound.* It's a phenomenon where the aircraft experiences a sudden increase in aerodynamic drag and other undesirable effects when approaching the speed of 767mph. In early attempts to break it, aircraft would experience severe aerodynamic buffeting as it approached the speed they would have to cancel the program for safety reasons.

The same rules apply in the spirit in our prayer time. As you start to pray with real determination, you are entering into a war zone, carnal against the spirit, persevering to the mark. I see this as the sound barrier. It is why Jesus in the Garden of Gethsemane, just before He reached the breakthrough mark, went through so much pressure and turbulence. A massive attack from the enemy. Then He persevered through the barrier to smooth sailing on the other side when He was able to surrender His will to the Father. So, just before you get your breakthrough in prayer, all hell will break loose. Just stay on your knees and stand your ground to win.

"But thou, when thou prayest, enter into thy closet, and when thou hast shut the door, Pray to thy Father which is in secret; and thy Father which seeth in secret shall reward thee openly."
Matthew 6:6 (KJV)

So, it sounds like the Lord is telling us the *third key is to enter a prayer closet. A quiet place, to shut the door from all distractions outside.*

"And it came to pass in those days, that he went out into a mountain to pray and continued all night in prayer to God."
Luke 6:12 (KJV)

And the result of this was that Jesus was able to make a very important decision about choosing His 12 disciples. That's a big one! The Bible says He went out to a mountain to pray, a quiet place away from distractions and people. All night, which could be up to twelve hours, praying to the Father. When the Lord broke through, it was *early hours of the morning*. To that holy place, all night must seem like just an hour. So Jesus had to battle against self, just like we have to today.

The fourth key is that you have *to be hungry and thirsty for God's presence*. It is a known fact that we can go many days without food, but we need water daily to survive. And if we don't get it, we will get very thirsty and start to dehydrate. When you get a drink, it tastes like the best drink in the world. So the Lord responds to hunger:

"O God, thou art my God; early will I seek thee: my soul thirsteth for thee, my flesh longeth for thee in a dry and thirsty land, where no water is." Psalms 63:1(KJV)

It's getting to a point when only God's amazing presence will satisfy you. Another powerful one in this verse is, 'early will I seek you'. This to me means seeking the Lord in the early hours of the morning, a time when everyone is sleeping and with total quietness and peace, no distractions.
And I thought to myself why did David say in a dry and thirsty land, where there's no water?
I believe he's talking about not natural water but spiritual water, you only get in the presence of God.

Another secret I've noticed in seeking the Lord is that we may not feel anything after ten or twenty minutes, no breakthrough, no presence. But if only you *stay on your knees, the longer you stay on your knees the more the carnal flesh is dying*, so the closer you're getting to the presence of God, until you hit breakthrough, amen, amen.

The Tabernacle prayer

Most people in the world pray every day. Either for their favorite football team to win, to win the lottery, maybe a promotion at work, or to be prosperous in life etc. The Bible says He will hear the prayer of the righteous.

"The LORD is far from the wicked: But he heareth the prayer of the righteous."
Proverbs 15:29 (KJV)

The Tabernacle prayer is how God originally intended for us to come into His presence, with a connection to heaven.

Then the Lord spoke to Moses:

"And let them make me a sanctuary; that I may dwell among them."
Exodus 25:8 (KJV)

So, there was a constant connection between *Heaven and Earth*. In Gods house, the Tabernacle, they knew exactly when to set out and when to camp. By day the cloud was permanently connected to the Tent of Meeting in the same way God wants with us, and fire by night. When it lifted, it's time to set out. The word says when the cloud covered the Tent of Meeting, and the glory of the Lord filled the Tabernacle. Even Moses was not able to enter the Tent of Meeting because the cloud settled upon it. And the full glory of the Lord filled the Tabernacle. When God said build me a sanctuary, He was talking about the Holy Trinity, Father, Son and Holy Spirit, working in perfect unity together.

Everywhere in the Tabernacle you can see evidence of this. Like God said to Moses to anoint the Tent of Meeting, and everything in it, the Ark of the

Covenant; the table and all utensils; lampstand and utensils; the Altar of Incense, the Altar of Burnt Offering and utensils; the Laver and the priest. This anointing oil represents the Holy Spirit. All working together to worship God, only the priests with special permission were allowed in, like high priest Aaron, Moses' brother, and Aaron's sons. To minister unto the Lord, they had to take off their shoes before entering the Tabernacle. Wearing shoes symbolize restoration and reinstatement of status, in the ancient world, slaves often went barefoot, while free men wore shoes. So, because of sin mankind lost his status, and had to humble himself in the presence of holiness.

The priest was only allowed into the Holy of Holies, the place where the Ark of the Covenant resides, once a year, to sprinkle blood on the Mercy Seat, which was the lid of the Ark of the Covenant. Seven times, for a sin offering for the people,
How this relates to prayer is every believer in Christ, and through Jesus, the ultimate sacrifice for sin, has now given us full access to the most holy place, God's dwelling place, which is the presence of God. It's just as much alive today as it was then and lives in all of us by His Spirit. Every day in your prayer time it's a case of progressing to a different level in the Tabernacle. The Lord instructed Moses to build a large courtyard, inside the Tabernacle, which consisted of an *Altar of Sacrifice*, a *Laver,* and the Tent of Meeting, which contained the *lamp stands* and the *Table of Showbread,* or the bread of the presence. Most importantly, the Holy of Holies where the *Ark of the Covenant* was kept, **is** where the presence of God resides. God instructed Moses to make a *gate to enter in*; it was the only way in and out.

"Here I am! I stand at the door and knock. If anyone hears my voice and opens the door, I will come in and eat with that person, and they with me." Revelation 3:20(NIV)

You see, this is the start of salvation, when we first open the door to Jesus and make a decision to follow Him. He is the gate, the way, the access to the Tabernacle, and that leads to heaven. The Bible says He's the way to salvation.

"I am the way, the truth, and the life: no man cometh unto the Father but by me."
John 14:6 (KJV)

Jesus can only speak truth, and gives you new life to live, at the gate, for there's only one way to heaven, through Jesus Christ.

So, as I look back on my life, before I got saved, I used to pray sometimes to God, but with little results. I was praying outside the *Tabernacle*, it was a prayer without faith, it seems I was just praying for the sake of it. Like how most people pray in the world, you think if you approached someone in the street and asked them to buy you a car, motorbike or house, they would probably laugh at you and think you're crazy!

The fact is, they *don't know you*, and you don't know them, so what right do you have to ask for something? But if you were to ask your parents for something you desire, it would be a totally different story. The Bible says what parent who loves their child, asking for something, would give them a stone or nothing at all. To start with, your parents *know you*, and love you, so they will not withhold any good thing from you.

"For the LORD God is a sun and shield: The LORD will give grace and glory: No good thing will he withhold from them that walk uprightly."
Psalms 84:11 (KJV)

So, if we keep our walk clean, He's promised to take care of all our needs in life. The second thing is you're in a relationship with God, He is our Father who looks out for us continually, and knowing we are protected by love, which resembles the walls of the Tabernacle. Moses was instructed to put 60 pillars up surrounding the Outer Court, to keep it holy and sanctified. There's protection in true love from God when you start praying the Tabernacle prayer.

So, we go about our daily Christian life - going to work, shopping, driving down the road, etc. In the spirit world, there are holy witnesses that testify that we are blood-bought into the family of Christ.

"For there are three that bear record in heaven, the Father, the Word, and the Holy Ghost: and these three are one."
1 John 5:7 (KJV)

These are one in agreement. It's amazing, these powerful witnesses sit upon us daily, and still in prayer on our knees and have victory over the flesh. Amen! You're able to progress from the Gate to the *Laver*. God spoke to Moses to make a Laver - a big bowl made of solid brass and filled with water for the priests to wash their hands and feet before they went about doing duties in the Tabernacle or they would die.

"They made the bronze basin and its bronze stand from the mirrors of the women who served at the entrance to the tent of meeting."
Exodus 38:8 (NIV)

So, as the priest looked in the bowl, they would see their reflection. The water represents the Word of God, the living waters, refreshing our mind and soul. As we read the Word of God in faith in our prayer time, we *see our reflection like a mirror.* The Lord will start to reveal things to you in your life, by His Spirit, and start making adjustments.

"Anyone who listens to the word but does not do what it says is like someone who looks at his face in a mirror and, after looking at himself, goes away and immediately forgets what he looks like."
James 1:23 (NIV)

"And the Spirit and the bride say, Come. And let him that heareth say, Come. And let him that is athirst come. And whosoever will, let him take the water of life freely."
Revelation 22:17(KJV)

This is anyone who wishes to take the *free gift of the water of life*. Jesus is the healing waters that cleanses you.

All the priests who ministered in the Tabernacle wore long garments with no shoes, barefoot to still remind them they're walking on holy ground. To honour the Lord, with their steps. The washing of their hands to remind them of their work for the Lord must remain clean. The Word says, "Ye are clean but not all", so in other words, you are only halfway there, and the washing of their feet, showing them that their walk must remain clean.
"When I washed my steps with butter, and the rock poured me out rivers of oil."
Job 29:6 (KJV)

So, I believe that Jesus, the water of the Word, can affect the steps you take, and Holy Spirit guiding you to the right places to go, because He's washing your steps clean with His holy water, amen.

"I will sprinkle clean water on you, and you will be clean; I will cleanse you from all your impurities and from all your idols."
Ezekiel 36:25 (NIV)

So, as you see your reflection, you see yourself in the Word of God, the Bible. This is the time when your prayer starts to come *alive* and you're starting to touch on the *power of the Word.* How it starts to influence your walk with God, and as your hands are washed the Word of God, it starts to influence the work you do. It starts taking on a new meaning because of the washing of the Word.

I love it, so your time in God's presence keeps getting deeper and deeper.

"And the LORD shall guide thee continually, and satisfy thy soul in drought, and make fat thy bones: And thou shalt be like a watered garden, and like a spring of water, whose waters fail not."
Isaiah 58:11(KJV)

I think it's amazing at this stage the Word of God starts to change you!!

"The law of the LORD is perfect, converting the soul:
The testimony of the Lord is sure, making wise the simple."
Psalms 19:7(KJV)

The law of the Lord is truly perfect. Your love is so amazing Lord. Still in prayer...what is prayer?

Prayer is:

Confession.

Supplication.

Adoration.

Intimacy.

Intercession.

Thanksgiving.

Praise.

Surrender.

Honour.

Confession - We pray according to the Word of God and confess His word, You've said Lord."
Supplication - A plea, making your request known to God in His presence.
Adoration - A time of loving God, and worshiping Him, for who He is.
Intimacy - Enter that deep place with God, loving Him.
Intercession - Where the Holy Spirit intercedes for you (Romans 8:26).
Thanksgiving - Giving thanks for everything in beauty of Holiness.
Praise - Lifting up His name in praise, and honour.
Surrender - We surrender our will to God.
Honour - We honour the Lord for who He is.

Still in prayer, you come past the Laver. As you progress, you move to *the Altar of Sacrifice*, made from shittim wood, overlaid with brass, and with four horns on each corner. As a sin offering, the priest would sprinkle blood on the horns of it. This speaks of death and the shedding of blood. I dare say there's a many Christians still at this stage and unable to progress in their prayer life, because still no blood cleansing to their spirit, and may be for years in the same position. This is when you surrender your flesh, the carnal side of man to be crucified. The side that thinks he doesn't need Gods help, laying aside all the pride and self-will, on the altar.

I believe what you feed something that's what it will grow into, like a young child growing up. The language being spoken around them, TV, social media, friends they keep, entertainment, etc., that's what they will become.

"There is therefore now no condemnation to them which are in Christ Jesus, who walk not after the flesh, but after the Spirit."
Romans 8:1 (KJV)

"For to be carnally minded is death; but to be spiritually minded is life and peace."
Romans 8:6(KJV)

So, then they that are in the flesh cannot please God. So, at this stage the Lord wants, through the Holy Spirit, for the carnal side to die. This is a place of death to self, because from the days of Adam and Eve, this body has already been cursed. Every day when we wake up there's a battle raging for our soul. The battle is flesh versus the spirit. So, as you start to get the victory over your flesh, it will elevate you to this stage of prayer, the supernatural blood that Jesus had shed and sacrificed on the cross for us.

As Christ wore the crown of thorns on His head. I believe to be *'euphoria milii'*. It was highly toxic because its milky juice contains a toxin called phorbol ester. Phorbol esters can irritate the skin after contact with the human body, and ingestion can cause severe stomach pain, throat and oral irritation, and vomiting. Jesus soaked it in much pain and blood for us. The toxic poison in the crown represents the curse of satan, that comes to attach in your mind. With all kinds of negativity, doubts, fears, stress etc.

"For God hath not given us the spirit of fear; but of power, and of love, and of a sound mind."
2 Timothy 1:7 (KJV)

But we can rejoice because Jesus has given us the victory, amen. All this pain He acquired, to win the battle for us, and anybody who will call upon His name in faith. The blood will start to cleanse your mind of every thought that does not line up with the Word of God. So, it is letting the blood of Christ cleanse us *daily* from all our sins, and our guilt and shame. Not natural blood but supernatural blood. Cleanse us from all secret faults in our lives and everything that is not of God. Cleanse us all today, Lord. You see, it's also the blood that defeats darkness, the evil forces, the devil. It's supernatural blood, *the devil sees it*, and is fearful of it, and will not come near it; he will pass you by, he won't come near you! The blood to the devil is like in the movie, 'Superman', kryptonite, it destroys Him!!!!!

"And the blood shall be to you for a token upon the houses where ye are: and when I see the blood, I will pass over you, and the plague shall not be upon you to destroy you, when I smite the land of Egypt."
Exodus 12:13 (KJV)

This shows me that when the enemy sees this, he will not come near you or your household.
He remembers it's the very thing that defeated him over two thousand years ago, on the cross. So, we are totally victorious over the enemy, we're seated with Christ in high places.

"Far above all principality, and power, and might, and dominion, and every name that is named, not only in this world, but also in that which is to come."
Ephesians 1:21 (KJV)

As you progress in prayer from the Altar of Sacrifice, you move to the Tent of Meeting. Welcome to this amazing place of revelation in prayer. This is a deep place with God, where He is guaranteed to meet with you. Everything inside got a symbolic meaning, where you start to experience a revealing of the glory of God in a way that you've never experienced before. I believe every time the priest came into the Tent of Meeting to minister unto the Lord, it was a new experience.

"And be renewed in the spirit of your mind; and that ye put on the new man, which after God is created in righteousness and true holiness."
Ephesians 4:23-24 (KJV)

Everyone loves something new, maybe a new house, new car, buying new clothes etc., but here the Lord is saying, "I'm restoring your mind your soul, everything about you is coming new."

"He maketh me to lie down in green pastures: He leadeth me beside the still waters. He restoreth my soul."
Psalms 23 2-3 (KJV)

There was a constant connection to heaven here. The Bible says by day a cloud permanently went up to heaven and fire by night. If it lifted, the camp would move on. The tent was made up of ten curtains, and the frame was made of acacia wood and covered in pure gold. While all the furniture in the outer court was bronze, in the Tent of Meeting, it was all gold. It's divine.

I think it's amazing, even though Jesus had not gone to the cross yet, it was already decided by God in advance over three thousand years before. Evidence of this is in the pattern given to Moses on the mount. For example, one of the coverings instructed to use was *goat's hair*, I believe this represents Lord Jesus as a sin bearer, who came in the likeness of sinful flesh (He Himself not sinless). The covering was of hair of a goat, not the skin. Suggesting that the sacrifice had not yet been offered yet, but pointing to it, many years in the future. It is why the Lord says Revelation 1:8, I am Alpha and Omega, the beginning and the ending, saith the Lord.
Everything is planned ahead it time, just like our lives, it's a book, with different chapters. He knows your beginning and ending, it's all a walk of faith and trust. Another covering used was a *ram's skin dyed red*. The significance of the ram's skin dye, in this, we see Christ in all the energy of perfect life and through the love He has for us all. Yielding it up at the cross, the skin turned red showing all the blood that was shed. In death as the ultimate sacrifice, in total devoutness to God and this marked His entire course here.

The next covering above was *badger's skin*. The significance suggests to me the nakedness of the skin. Represents Jesus Christ, hanging there on the cross. Alone, despised, ridiculed, spat upon, and mocked. More of all, it was a site of shame. It was exposing the essence of the self that needs to be hidden. This skin, compared to a ram's skin, lacked beauty. He paid the price through the suffering to reign in victory over the devil.

God said to Moses to make five poles at the entrance to the Tent of Meeting, I believe this represents the five-fold ministries.

"And he gave some, apostles; and some, prophets; and some, evangelists; and some, pastors and some teachers; for the perfecting of the saints, for the work of the ministry, for the edifying of the body of Christ."
Ephesians 4:11-12 (KJV)

So, as the Lord leads you in this deep place of prayer, He starts revealing a fresh side to Him through the Holy Spirit into ministry, serving Him, a place of surrender to His will. The results of these five ministries touching your life are."
- Honour - Develop a new deep honour for the Lord.
- Maturity - You will be mature in everything you do and speak.
- The Lord will establish you as a force to be reckoned with.
- You will be rooted and grounded in the faith, unmovable.
- Free from deception - Be able to see through the devil's plans for your life.
- Be able to speak truth in love with power from God.

The Lord instructed Moses to make a lamp stand, made of solid gold with seven branches. The priest was to use olive oil for the light, and place it on the south side of the house. As the priest would enter the Tent of Meeting, the whole house would be in complete darkness. So, that's why God instructed Moses to keep the lamp stand burning 24 hours a day. In the same way, Jesus requires us to keep our lamps of faith burning constantly all day, no matter what situation we're going through.

The priest would minister unto the Lord first thing in the morning and evening.
"O God, thou art my God; early will I seek thee: My soul thirsteth for thee, my flesh longeth for thee in a dry and thirsty land, where no water is." Psalms 63:1 (KJV)

So, still intoxicated in prayer with the glory of the Lord filling your room, it's amazing as you read now, the Word of God, it just starts to come alive. The lamp stand is now radiating with the light and glory, bringing you pure revelation by the Holy Spirit.

"Be exalted, O God, above the heavens; let your glory be over all the earth." Psalm 57:5 (NIV)

Be thou exalted, O God, above the heavens, let thy glory be above all the earth. At the lamp stand, it's praise taken to a higher level. The darker the situation, the more the light of the Lord will come through, lighting your path.

"But the path of the just is as the shining light, That shineth more and more unto the perfect day." Proverbs 4:18 (KJV)

So, as we continue each day in Christ Jesus, our path is getting brighter and brighter to that perfect day when we see Jesus in glory. What a day that will be, I say, "Come Lord Jesus, I anticipate your return."

God instructed Moses to place the table of shewbread opposite the lampstands. It was made of shittim wood covered with pure gold, and to keep the bread of the presence on it, 24 hours a day.

Two stacks of six loaves represent the 12 tribes of Israel. God instructed the priest to pour frankincense over the bread. As the cloud of glory fills the place, at this stage, I'm normally in tears, running down my face, giving thanks and praise to God. The bread represents the Word of God.

"And Jesus answered him, saying, It is written, That man shall not live by bread alone, But by every word of God."
Luke 4:4 (KJV)

So, this is spiritual food. As we read the Word of God, we are no longer hungry but satisfied, and because of our experiencing the Word of God, the frankincense poured on it gave the Word of God a sweet smell, but a bitter taste. This means the revelation of the Word of God brings persecution and problems from the enemy. Everywhere you go, you're carrying a fragrance of praise that only comes from an intimate place of God's Amazing presence.

"If ye be reproached for the name of Christ, Happy are ye, for the spirit of glory and of God resteth upon you: on their part he is evil spoken of, but your part he is glorified."
1 Peter 4:14 (KJV)

On their part, He is evil spoken of, but on your part, He is glorified. It's not nice being persecuted and treated unjustly, and oppressed by governmental people, for the name of Jesus Christ. This is what the disciples experienced in the Bible; it's a promise to all believers. Once you've experienced the revelation of the Word of God, it brings persecution. It's sometimes like the enemy unleashes trouble on every side, bombarding us with different attacks. It's because the glorious light of your life in the spirit world is *radiating, affecting everything.* From the moment we wake up in the morning, there's a battle raging for our souls. It's painful going through these things. Jesus went through it all. He endured. He pressed through the pain. I believe every challenge and problem has a time limit, and if we endure, keep pressing, never giving up, we will win over darkness. But we must remember that when the devil comes to attack us in terms of authority, he is beneath us.

"Which he wrought in Christ, when he raised him from the dead, and set him at his own right hand in the heavenly places, far above all principality, and power, and might, and dominion, and every name that is named, not only in this world, but also in that which is to come."
Ephesians 1:20-21 (KJV)

The level of authority goes as follows:
- God the Father in heavenly places.
- The born-again believer, we are seated with Christ.
- Angels of God.
- Satan's dominion.
- The unsaved person.

So, when the devil comes to attack, they're on a relentless, organised mission, and their sole purpose is to steal, kill and destroy. To win, you first must *know your position* of authority and the weapons available to you to defeat and annihilate his camp.

The enemy is a deceiver, and his tactics have not changed over thousands of years. When he's attacking, his common deception is to pretend he's got authority over the believer, but the truth is he's beneath our feet. The Lord Jesus stripped him of his authority many years ago, at the cross when He gave His life.

"And having disarmed the powers and authorities, he made a public spectacle of them, triumphing over them by the cross."
Colossians 2:15 (NIV)

I like this phrase, *disarmed*, which means to take away a weapon or weapons from a person, force or country. So, the enemy has been permanently stripped of its arsenal. The phrase powers and authorities refers to the demonic forces that oppose God and seek to dominate humanity.

The Lord made a *public spectacle* of them, suggesting that Jesus had exposed and humiliated these demonic forces, making them visible and recognisable as defeated. In our current day would be all over headline news on TV, would have gone viral on the internet, social media, and around the world. Everyone would have seen them defeated.

"For we wrestle not against flesh and blood, but against principalities, against powers, against the rulers of darkness of this world, against spiritual wickedness in high places."
Ephesians 6:12 (KJV)

So, when attacks and problems arise could be at work or at home, etc., it's easy to think people are the problem, because that's what your natural eyes can see. The truth is the devil loves to hide behind something, disguise his true identity, just like with Adam and Eve in Eden. The enemy came to deceive in the form of a snake, but as the Word says, we wrestle not against people, flesh and blood, but in the spirit world against principalities. Which means a small territory ruled by a prince, powers, and rulers, and conveys authority. These fallen angels are ruled by satan. *Spiritual wickedness* in high places is the twisted, evil spirits that lie, deceive, and orchestrate the wickedness, twisted perversion that takes place on earth.

So, I say now, in battle, I'm happy to go through it because I'm promised the spirit of glory and of God will rest upon me. Be encouraged today, God is on your side in the heat of the battle.

"What shall we then say to these things? If God be for us, who can be against us?"
Romans 8:31 (KJV)

As the presence of the Lord continues to fill the room in prayer, there's a wonderful fragrance going up from *the Altar of Incense*. God instructed Moses to construct and make of shittim wood, covered with pure gold, with four horns. Aaron the priest was instructed to place it before the veil and burn sweet-smelling incense every morning and evening, when he dressed the lamps. The priest was also ordered to only take the fire from the Altar of Sacrifice. *Do not bring strange fire* to the altar of Incense, or you will die. I believe the significance of this, God gave the fire, which lit the hot coals coming only from the Altar of Sacrifice, which represented the blood sacrifice for sins. So, as your prayer goes up like incense to the Lord, it's justified now by the blood that Jesus has shed on the cross, and because the house of meeting is a holy place. There was a constant connection to heaven. So, an unauthorised prayer, a strange fire, offered, brings instant judgment, this is what happened to two priests, Aaron's two sons.

"And Nadab and Abihu, the sons of Aaron, took either of them his censer, and put fire therein, and put incense thereon, and offered strange fire before the LORD, which he commanded them not. And there went out fire from the LORD, and devoured them, and they died before the LORD."
Leviticus 10:1-2 (KJV)

I believe this happened because the sin of man had not yet been covered yet by Jesus, so no grace and mercy. Also in our holy prayer time, the Lord is the only one who brings fire to your sacrifice, and light it up before people, amen.

Once a year, on the horns, Aaron was to make an atonement with the blood of the sin offering for the people. So, as the wonderful presence of God continues, your prayers go up as sweet-smelling incense, a wonderful aroma fills your room.

"Let my prayer be set forth before thee as incense; And the lifting up of my hands as the evening sacrifice."
Psalm 141:2 (KJV)

The fire of God radiates a constant connection up to heaven in the spirit, taking your prayer sacrifice to heaven. The Lord inhabits the praises of His people, so as the priest would burn the incense over the fire, the smoke of praise would fill the whole house and the Holy of Holies, elevating your prayer to a deeper place where the presence of the Lord resides.

There was a veil separating the *Holy of Holies.* Moses was instructed to make an Ark of the Covenant made of shittim wood and cover it with pure gold. The carrying poles were never to be removed, unlike the rest of the furniture. Inside the Ark was a golden pot that had manna, Aaron's rod that budded, and the tablets of the covenant, the Ten Commandments. Once a year, the priest would sprinkle blood on the Mercy Seat for the sins of the people.

This is the place of praise and revelation, where only God is exalted. This was the real meeting place that heaven would connect to earth. In prayer one day, this reminded me of my first experience with salvation. When I was in the presence of the Lord and He spoke to me, I was on my bedroom floor for over five hours. But it only felt like 30 minutes; this was a transition from Earth's time to no time, Heaven's rules.

"Now the man Moses was very meek, above all the men which were upon the face of the earth."
Numbers 12:3 (KJV)

"And the LORD spake unto Moses face to face, as a man speaketh unto his friend. And he turned again into the camp, but His servant Joshua, the son of Nun, a young man, departed not out of the Tabernacle."
Exodus 33:11 (KJV)

So, the Lord was able to speak to his face. This shows me that when you progress to this level of prayer, the presence of God is so tangible and sweet. Just like Joshua in the glory, when it was time to leave, he just couldn't. It was like a magnet pulling him to stay, so he stayed there in the glorified presence. He did not want to return to reality. I believe there was a transition from Earth's time to *Heaven's atmosphere and rules*, where there's no time and no natural sun. The true light and Glory of God would illuminate the most holy place. The veil separated the Tent of Meeting, which means the lampstand, the only source of light, was in the next room. The Word of God says in His full glory, no man was able to enter the Tent of Meeting. So God lifted most of His glory just for human flesh could enter in and not die.

"Then a cloud covered the tent of the congregation, and the glory of the LORD filled the Tabernacle. And Moses was not able to enter into the tent of congregation."
Exodus 40:34-35 (KJV)

I believe that the glory of God in its fullness could not accommodate sin in mankind, because Jesus's life had not been offered sacrifice yet, for sin, and the law of sin and death still ruled. The grace of God had yet to be given, the priest had to wear bells on their garment, so if the bell stopped, everyone would know something was wrong in the presence of the Lord, and they might need rescuing. So, let's thank the Lord for His grace and steadfast love, giving us all now full access to the most holy place.

"O God thou art My God; early will I seek thee; My soul thirsteth for thee, my flesh longeth for thee in a dry and thirsty land, where no water is; To see thy power and thy glory, So as I have seen thee in the sanctuary. Because thy lovingkindness is better than life, My lips shall praise thee. Thus will I bless thee while I live: I will lift up my hands in thy name. My soul shall be satisfied as with marrow and fatness; And my mouth shall praise thee with joyful lips."
Psalm 63:1-5 (KJV)

This is the place in prayer where your soul is truly *satisfied, not thirsty anymore*. Your spirit is whole, complete, because God's holy presence brings peace and satisfaction, but more than anything, at this stage, it's *revelation* where everything comes alive!!

So, as I continued in prayer and experienced the revelation of God, tears fell down my face.
In glory to God and awe of His glorious presence, that sweet-smelling incense starts to rise to heaven. It's why when we come out of prayer, we've still got the fragrance of praise and glory on us, radiating that sweet-smelling incense. When Moses came out of the presence of God the glory of God was so strong on Him, he had to put a veil on His face because it was shining like the sun. That's the glory of God. I think the closer you get to God, the more of His glory rubs off on us, more than we realise. It's what we all need in these last days to defeat satans domain. We need the glory and the power of God to bring down strongholds in our lives and the people around us.
"Deep calleth unto deep at the noise of thy waterspouts: All thy waves and thy billows are gone over me."
Psalms 42:7(KJV)

This is a deep place in the spirit, like a deep ocean in prayer, when you take the strongholds of life that have been holding you, your family members or anyone else you know, for a long time. Take them, not just down, but from, the root of the problem. At this stage in prayer, the Lord will start revealing things to you and bringing you in close union with the Father. Let the same mind of Christ be in you. As Paul says in:

"For who hath known the mind of the Lord, that he may instruct him? But we have the mind of Christ."
1 Corinthians 2:16 (KJV)

So, in past times, the priest would have to intercede for the people in the Tabernacle for sin. But now, because Jesus paid the price for us, cleared our debt of sin, conquered the grave and rose victoriously, we all as believers can have full access to His holy presence of the Tabernacle prayer, while the Holy Spirit now intercedes for us in prayer. So, this is the only way to live your life, with the presence of God filling you and guiding you through every situation. Praise God.

Jacob's time in God's presence

I believe our destiny in the eyes of the Lord is already written, like a book. Each day of our lives reads a different chapter.

"Now the just shall live by faith: But if any man draw back, my soul shall have no pleasure in him."
Hebrews 10:38 (KJV)

Which means we don't know what's waiting around the next corner or what tomorrow holds. It is why we have to learn to trust the Lord. It was the same in Jacob's life when his grandfather Abraham only gave a vague instruction to his servant to find a wife for Isaac.

"And my master made me swear, saying, Thou shalt not take a wife to my son of the daughters from the Canaanites, in whose land I dwell: but thou shalt go unto my Father's house, and to my kindred, and take a wife unto my son."
Genesis 24:37-38 (KJV)

It was all the instructions given. It was a walk of faith. It's the same sometimes in our lives. We're believing the Lord for something, and He only gives you the first step in the process. Just like how the Lord told me to put pen to paper and write this book. I was working for a bookshop at the time, delivering books, just me in the shop. In the early hours of the morning, the Lord said, "Looking up at all these best sellers on the shelf, you will have a book up here titled, 'The Amazing Presence of God, ' declaring to the nations, it's a walk of faith." Because I knew nothing about writing or how to go about it, I just received the first step in the process.

"Before I formed thee in the belly, I knew thee; and before thou camest forth out of the womb I sanctified thee, and I ordained thee a prophet unto the nations."
Jeremiah 1:5 (KJV)

It's the same with Jacob's life, where greatness is coming in the family line. There's always a great war in the spirit world. For example, Rebecca, Isaac's wife, was barren; there was a battle going on in the spirit for the birth of Jacob. The real war. If Satan senses danger and a threat to his demonic kingdom, he will form a weapon. The Lord spoke to Jacob in His presence confirming saying, "And thy seed shall be as the dusk of the Earth and thou shalt spread abroad to the west and to the east and to the north and to the south in thee and thy seed shall all the families of the Earth be blessed."
And it was this same seed that Jesus came through, so the promise was locked up in the spirit.
"And Isaac intreated the LORD for his wife, because she was barren: and the LORD was intreated of him and Rebekah his wife conceived."
Genesis 25:21(KJV)
The Lord had to come in and break the curse to release the promise. I believe our personalities are already shaped before conception.

"And the children struggled together within her; and she said, If it be so, why am I thus? And she went to enquire of the LORD.
Genesis 25:22(KJV)

Two completely different personalities, Jacob, a spiritual man, Esau a carnal man. They both had different goals in life. Jacob just desired and hungered after things of a spiritual nature, with a strong desire in life to be blessed of the Lord, and to come into His holy presence.

"The first to come out was red, and his whole body was like a hairy garment; so they named him Esau. After this, his brother came out, with his hand grasping Esau's heel; so he was named Jacob. Isaac was sixty years old when Rebekah gave birth to them."
Genesis 25:25-26 (KIV)

So, to me, Jacob's one desire was to be blessed and to spend time in God's amazing presence. No matter what it cost him, he was willing to pay the price.

"Blessed are they which do hunger and thirst after righteousness: for they shall be filled."
Matthew 5:6 (KJV)

I believe this is one of God's laws that will, without doubt, bring you into the presence of God, and that's hunger and thirst. The Lord would say to you today, "How hungry are you for My presence? Are you willing to pay the price Jacob was like this growing up? He had a strong desire to come into the presence of God, but did not know how to go about it, did not have an instruction manual, and this flesh was battling with the spirit. When the balance is wrong, we try and help God to put our own plan into action, to acquire the goal, usually with disastrous results and consequences. Just like when Rebecca, his mum, joined forces with Jacob to defraud his brother Esau out of his birthright.

The law of hunger and thirst was already there. What Jacob had from the start, but went through these desert times in his life, when it was not producing any fruit or any visible results. Like all of us in different situations of life, we just have to trust the Lord and wait. We serve a righteous God and who is truthful.

"God is a Spirit: and they that worship him must worship him in spirit and truth."
John 4:24 (KJV)

The devil, like a snake, came in the flesh of Jacob's vulnerability and weakness to bring in deception and fraud and lies. In life, the enemy can mask himself and entice you to do a good thing, but it's the wrong thing. Even in them days, the tradition was that the firstborn would get the blessing, but God was able to give the blessing to Jacob without deception, opening a door to evil plans.

Despite everything that had happened, in Genesis 28:1, Isaac called Jacob and blessed him. So, with threats coming from his brother to kill him, he left his family home to start a new life.

"The steps of a good man are ordered by the LORD: And he delighteth in his way."
Psalm 37:23 (KJV)

So, I believe because he loved the Lord and hungered and thirst for Him that his steps were ordered by the Lord. *Jacob's first real encounter* in the presence of the Lord.

"And he dreamed, and behold a ladder set up on the earth, and the top of it reached to heaven: and behold the angels of God ascending and descending on it. And, behold, the LORD stood above it, and said I am the LORD God of Abraham thy Father, and the God of Isaac."
Genesis 28:12-13 (KJV)

So, in this chapter of Jacob's life, the Lord chose to make His appearance. Jacob's flesh was slowly dying, to deception, selfishness and wrong thinking.

The Lord did not reveal Himself to his brother Esau because no real hunger and thirst for the presence of God.

"And the boys grew: and Esau was a cunning hunter, a man of the field; and Jacob was a plain man, dwelling in tents."
Genesis 25:27 (KJV)

Most probably studying the Word of God. As Jacob continued in his life and walk with the Lord, there were still unresolved problems that had not been addressed from the past, that had not been put right. With the same thought on his mind, like a heavy weight.

"Then Jacob was greatly afraid and distressed." Genesis 32:7. The enemy was using the situation to bring every evil thought into his head of what could go wrong.

With the meeting of his brother, the Lord says, "Before we come into prayer, if there's unforgiveness, go and make right before we come into the presence of God." Many years had passed, and I don't think there was one single day that went past he did not think about the situation with his brother. Through the stress of it all, Jacob that night sent His family ahead of him. He could not bear the thought of it any longer, it was just too much.

"And Jacob was left alone; and there wrestled a man with him until the breaking of day. And when he saw that he prevailed not against him, he touched a hollow of his thigh; and the hollow of Jacob's thigh was out of joint, as he wrestled with him. And he said, Let me go, for the day breaketh. And he said, I will not let thee go, except thou bless me. And he said unto him, What is thy name? And he said, Jacob. And he said, Thy name shall be called no more Jacob, but Israel: for as a prince hast thou power with God and with men, and hast prevailed."

Genesis 32:24-28 (KJV)

This, to me, was the big showdown fight. The flesh against the spirit. This fight would decide Jacob's future. The strategy of the enemy has not changed over the years, and just before we get a breakthrough, he would turn up with an army to bring a heavy weight of distress and problems. To try and hinder progress. The second thought is the word *"alone."* He was left alone. This could resemble a desert situation in your life. Seems like everything has dried up, no results, no breakthroughs, nothing, just dead work. It means you're very close to the breakthrough

It's when the lord is ready to make an appearance in your life. He wrestled with an angel till the break of day in the spirit world. It's still the spirit fighting against the flesh because the Lord wants to crucify the flesh, so He has more room to come in to give us more power to fight. Another key which Jacob had was the word *"determination."* He was determined enough in his life to never give up the passion, the hunger, the zeal for the presence of God.

"And he said, 'Let me go, for the day breaketh. And he said, I will not let thee go, except thou bless me."
Genesis 32:26 (KJV)

Most people would have given up a long time ago or would have just lost their hunger for the presence of the Lord. When the angel came and changed his name from Jacob to Israel and said, "As a prince has power with God and with men and has prevailed." It was at this point that Jacob's flesh died, and the spirit of God took over and transformed him into a different person, with a new identity, giving him power to bring down strongholds. The last word I'd like to bring up is *"remember"*. The angel touched his thigh, and it became out of joint. So, the Lord wanted him to remember and to celebrate what had happened on that day and place.

I believe in our own personal lives, behind the scenes, there's always activity going on in the spirit world. The Word says, "Angels encamp around them. " Even in a simple task of just walking out to the shops, or just driving to work to get to where we're going safely without an incident, is a miracle, a divine intervention. The Lord is constantly fighting for you, because if the devil could have his way, he would take you out straight away. So, when he gives you a viable miracle like receiving a physical healing, a breakthrough in your career, promotion at work, a near miss on the road, etc., we should *remember* it, like Jacob did, by marking that place in your life, and give God the glory.

Being a witness at work

Being a witness is something every believer can do. It's just a case of letting your light shine and letting the Word of God come to you, and as it comes through you. The word "gospel" comes from a Greek word *'euangelion'*, which literally means "good news." When we turn on our TV seems to be majority "bad news," someone being killed, taken hostage, starvation in some parts of the world, wars, lies, deceit, and so on. Look at all the trouble news channels go through to get the live news to you. They send reporters all around the world to try and get that exclusive story to you. They would need to transmit a signal via satellite, fibre optic, or internet connectivity to the television station or online platform. They monitor and control it, in the studio with a team of people who edit programs, then send it to your TV sets.

I'm not saying all news is bad news on TV, but it seems we live in a world where bad news seems to sell more. You pick up a newspaper, and the majority seems to be bad news, but things don't have to be like this. I think it's fear of change. So, you think we have this great news, the gospel, the "good news" to tell the world how Jesus has changed our lives. You think the media goes through all that trouble to get the majority news to you, how much more can we do with the real good news. The Bible says:

"Ye are the light of the world. A city that is set on an hill cannot be hid. Neither do men light a candle, and put it under a bushel, but on a candlestick; and it giveth light unto all that are in the house. Let your light so shine before men, that they may see your good works, and glorify your Father which is in heaven."
Matthew 5:14-16 (KJV)

It's a desperate world out there, where people need the love of God in their lives. I was at work one day, not long after being saved and working as a skilled baker, but it felt like I was there for more reasons than just work. One day, I went on a lunch break in the canteen as I did every day and sat down to have lunch at the table. There was a young lady who worked in a different department whom I vaguely knew, she looked really fed up with life. Then I felt a burning desire from the Lord to witness to her. I thought to myself, "I can't do this, Lord. You must be joking, Lord, there are four other people at the table and the canteen is full of people." This fear just rose up in me, but I had this amazing experience of how I got saved, and I just had to share it with someone, so I built up the courage. I started by saying, "Did you know Jesus loves you?" Once these three words were spoken, I felt the Holy Spirit turn up *like fire*, the same feeling I felt in my bedroom on my knees, I was feeling in the canteen. I remembered:

"The spirit of the Lord spoke by me and His word was in my tongue."
2 Samuel 23:2

After the first few words were spoken to her, the rest of it started to flow like a river flowing from my mouth,

"He that believeth on me, as the scripture hath said, out his belly shall flow rivers of living water."
John 7:38

So let your rivers flow Lord, You're so amazing!! I carried on saying, "Jesus loves you, yes you, so much it goes past our understanding, so receive it today!" I then explained to her in Genesis 2:7 that the Lord God formed man from the dust of the ground and breathed into his nostrils the breath of life, and man became a living soul.

Then I said to her, "Breathe in, now breathe out, what do you feel?" She said, "Breath?" "That's it! You've got it!" I explained you can't escape from God because the breath in you is the life of God. Then the Spirit of the Lord led her to open her heart to me. She then explained how she has been really depressed lately and considered suicide. I told her suicide is not a way out, you think the grass is greener on the other side.

The Bible says:
"And as it is appointed unto men once to die, but after this the judgment." Hebrews 9:27 (KJV)

I carried on saying to her that if someone decides to end their life in this world, it's not that just their body that goes to the ground, but their spirit will live on. I see death as being absent from this earthly body. Paul in the Bible experienced what it is to be absent from the body in 2 Corinthians 12:3, "And I knew such a man, whether in the body or out of the body I cannot tell God knoweth." I think it must be like walking into another room, you will still feel touch, smell, see and so on. I continued saying, in 2 Corinthians 5:8, it says we are confident, I say, willing rather to be absent from the body is present with the Lord. Then I said to her to just trust Jesus with her life and that He would turn things around to work in her favour because of the love He has for her.

After saying this, I felt something break in the spirit realm. The Word of God was starting to take effect as she started to weep uncontrollably. *As the presence of the Lord filled where we were*, it was like a cloud came down and filled the room. Other people were there, but for a moment everyone dispersed, and a cloud surrounded us; there was a transformation taking place.

I said that we were all sinners in this world and Jesus came to redeem us from this sinful world. I asked whether she would like to make a commitment to follow Him, and open up your heart to let Him?

"Behold I stand at the door, and knock: if any man hear my voice, and open the door, I will come in to him, and will sup with him, and he with me."
Revelations 3:20 (KJV)

I continued to say Jesus is a perfect gentleman; He always knocks on the door. Even though He's always with you. You have to let Him in, and when you do, you will be amazed when the light comes in, you will start hearing a new tender voice of love, positivity and hope. She said, "I am willing to receive Him," and with tears she received Jesus right there at the canteen table at work, on my lunch hour. Praise God, you are so amazing, Lord.

The Word also says those who confess me before men, my Father will also confess in heaven. Now let's think about it for a second, Jesus the King of kings and Lord of lords, who made the Heavens and Earth, who sits far above principality and powers, the all mighty gracious, says, "Those who confess me on earth; My Father will confess your name in heaven." What a powerful statement!!!
I believe if we keep our walk clean with the Lord, His *word can not only come to us but also come through us.*

"When I washed my steps with butter, And the rock poured me out rivers of oil."
Job 29:6 (KJV)

I see "butter" as the wealthy part of the Word of God, the Bible, because butter comes from milk.

"As newborn babes, desire the sincere milk of the word, that ye may grow thereby."
1 Peter 2:2 (KJV)

So, when we first come to know the Lord, we start with the milk until he gives the *rhema* of the Word, directing our steps and the places we go. You think every step we take can be influenced by the butter of the Word of God; you will just have no desire to go to places which does not glorify God. The rock, which is Christ Jesus, the solid rock, is pouring out the oil of gladness and the anointing on your life. In Exodus, God commanded Moses to anoint every item in the Tabernacle with holy anointing oil. The Old Testament speaks of a shadow of things. Since Jesus came, we are now in the substance and His grace. The Lord pours out His Anointing oil where anyone who gets around anyone with the anointing, it's like a rubbing effect to transform with fresh oil. It's also like having a perfume or fragrance on you, and after speaking to someone, after you've left. They can still smell the fragrance on them, of praise. The Lord also says signs and wonders shall follow those who believe.

Being a witness is a commandment to all believers in Christ, so let your light so shine before men, it's still something we choose to do, because every person has free will. Jesus would never pressure anyone into doing anything they didn't want to do. When we look at what Jesus has done for us, saving us from a life of sin and death, why not share the good news? Even an act of kindness to someone is still bringing light to a dark place, I continued, saying to her.

To give you an example, say you just finished work and are on your way home, walking down the high street. A car with its brakes failed was heading towards you, and you did not notice it! And a stranger noticed the danger and, without thinking, dived out to save you and in doing so ended up losing their life to save you. You would be so grateful to that person who just saved your life. Life would take on a new meaning; you being alive would mean you owe your life to that person. Everyone you meet, you would want to tell them about this great person who saved your life, how much more for Christ. I tell you this, over two thousand years ago, Jesus chose to give His life to save us from eternal hell and destruction, because of the love which He has for us.

I only had 15 minutes left of lunch, and at this stage, Carol was in tears as the Lord was ministering to her. I gave another illustration. I said, look at the clothes you're wearing, and the cutlery on the tables, the television, also look at the cars outside, they all have one thing in common, they all have a creator. A car, for example, would probably start with an idea, turn that into a design model, then the real thing, and when you see the beautiful countryside where we live and how everything was formed. How could somebody possibly deny there's a creator? The Lord loves to create and design. He makes everything beautiful in His time, and He calls us all to worship and live in unity. I said all the stress and problems you're going through are only amplified because you're just hearing one voice, the tormentor. You will now start to hear a new voice, so let His love surround you and give you peace, amen. Lunch was over.

That's why I do not have a problem with sharing the Word of God with people. Sometimes I feel a bit nervous, but then I remember what Christ has done for me, and then it brings such confidence and boldness.

"For God hath not given us the spirit of fear; but of power, and of love, and of a sound mind. Be not thou therefore ashamed of the testimony of our Lord."
2 Timothy 1:7-8 (KJV)

I just want to tell the whole world about the goodness of God, so let's put the light of God on our rooftops where every person can see and hear. Praise to God.

Coming out of comfort zone

Coming out of familiarity, a comfort zone, is always hard, because everybody loves to be comfortable, like an armchair at home. In our minds, we like doing things that are familiar to do, and we get into a set routine. For example, at work we're acquainted with our colleagues, their behaviour, etc. Our job is done over and over repeatedly, so we get familiar with what we do. The job may offer great benefits, such as a pension and hopes of promotion in the future. When we are on our way home, we will take a familiar route. I believe the average person is fearful of risk and the unknown, we just like to be comfortable in what we're doing tomorrow and the future. At home, for most people, it will be a familiar situation as well. You may be used to your wife cooking a roast dinner on a Sunday, going to the gym on certain days of the week, etc. Our brain seems to be programmed to be in a set routine, and anything out of this seems a risky, shady area to be in.

Sometimes the Lord will call us out of our comfort zone to do a special job for Him.

"Now the LORD had said unto Abram, Get thee out of thy country, and from thy kindred and from thy father's house, unto a land that I will shew thee."
Genesis 12:1
It's a step of faith because there was no mention of where he's going.

You see, the Lord spoke to Abram to come out of familiarity because everything around him he was used to and accustomed to, like living in his father's house, he was still subject to the law of his father. So, in other words, Abram was limited in what the Lord could do for him; the blessing was too large to receive while staying where he was. All the Lord wanted was for him to trust Him on this new journey because the life of a Christian is a journey, from the moment you get saved to seeing Jesus in heaven. It's like a process to mould us and shape us like clay, so each day as we continue with Christ, it gets less of ourselves and more of Him. Jesus said His burden is light and His yoke is easy.

A story I heard a while back was about the growth of a fish, and that the growth of a fish is limited by the size of the tank or pond it lives in. So, the fish will never outgrow its surroundings. The same in our lives; it is like we all live in a cocoon and are limited until we step out in faith and out of familiarity. So, the Lord has to enlarge our surroundings before we can really grow and affect the world.

"For I will cast out the nations before thee, and enlarge thy borders."
Exodus 34:24 (KJV)

So, it's also enlarging the way we think and the way we see things, because the blessings and glory of God go past our understanding.

It was a familiar story with the life of Moses, where he had to come out of his comfort zone. His mum, Jochebed, when she saw that he was a godly child, hid him for 3 months. After that, the young child started to outgrow the surroundings, because she could no longer hide him anymore. Then this took real faith and courage. After placing him in a basket, she released Moses on the waters, knowing Pharaoh's daughter would regally bathe in the Nile at that time. So, the dream was now out of her hands, and now with the Holy Spirit, guiding and protecting him to his destination.

The same way we can have faith in our lives, whatever your passion or desire to accomplish is, or what you are believing God for, a lifelong dream may be, I tell you now, release the dream into the holy waters of God. Just trust Him and see what He will do, praise God. For me, my comfort zone was my job. I used to work for a large bookshop, and I was accustomed to seeing new books every morning coming in. The process of this continued for many months, and one day, I came into the shop as usual, early one morning. It was quiet and still, only me in the shop. I looked up on the bookshelf, it was lettered with autobiographies, novels, fiction, faith books, titles with all different well-known stars in the media.

Then the Holy Spirit spoke to me in a quiet voice, saying, "You can do better than these people for the Kingdom of God to bring people back into the presence of God. This is just some of what the public is reading about." So, I thought, let's throw out the fisherman's net of salvation and bring in souls for the kingdom of God. So, that's where it all started, just laying down my dreams on the waters of God and seeing what He will do.

So, my story goes a bit like a reference again to when the Lord spoke to Abram to 'come out of thy country' and comfort zone, to enlarge his borders. It was like that for me. I've spent most of my life being brought up in South London, and I was used to my surroundings. I had all my friends and family nearby. I spent over twenty years of my life living there; it was a comfort zone, and I did not know any different. I regularly felt a calling in my spirit to come out of this familiarity. There was something calling me somewhere else.

But not long after getting saved with the Lord, I felt it was a change of season for my life from God.
Sometimes on weekends, my wife and I would enjoy driving out of the busy city, through the country, to the seaside to visit family. We used to love driving down to the beach, and I remember feeling such peace just sitting on the beach, watching the waves come in and out again. Then a thought came to me.

"He maketh me to lie down in green pastures: He leadeth me besides the still waters."
Psalm 23:2 (KJV)
I felt the stillness of God just flowing over the ocean.

"And the earth was without form, and void; and darkness was upon the face of the deep. And the spirit of God moved upon the face of the waters."
Genesis 1:2 (KJV)

"And God said, 'Let the water under the heaven be gathered together unto one place, and let dry land appear: and it was so."
Genesis 1:9 (KJV)

I think the handiwork of God's creation is so amazing. When you see the beauty of the world around us, you can only give Him praise and honour. It was a hard decision to come out of the comfort zone of what you're used to all your life. So, we took the plunge too, and moved to the country and bought a house down on the coast. I found it strange at first living in a place where I did not know anyone and in strange surroundings, with some of the people looking at me a bit strangely. Probably because there's not a great mixture of people living down here.

The high street shops closed really early, compared to a busy town in London, where everything is lively and open till late. It felt like a ghost town. My brain was not used to this at all. I was set in my ways, and I thought, "What have I done? What am I doing here?" In my mind, I was still in the comfort zone of the busy city. It was a step of faith and just trusting in God to lead us, because starting any new thing is never easy. Then the Lord opened a door for a good job opportunity. It came along for both of us, and when I look back now and see that the Lord just kept opening doors of blessings on our lives.

And when I went to seek the Lord in prayer, it became so much more powerful, partly because there was quietness. No one to disrupt, no peer pressure, because people down here did not care about what car you drive, or the latest fashion clothes etc., like London. It's why I think the more things we can lay down in our lives, the more God can move and have more access to our lives.

Most of the hard work that Jesus did to bring Himself out of His comfort zone was accomplished in a solitary place, away from the hustle and bustle of life and people.

"And in the morning, rising up a great while before day, he went out, and departed into a solitary place, and there prayed."
Mark 1:35 (KJV)

So, enabling Him to accomplish break breakthrough from the flesh into the supernatural, where the Holy Spirit went to work, like in the morning after Jesus chose His twelve disciples. This was all done through prayer and determination to succeed.

I believe God's desire for our lives is to come out of our comfort zone and bear fruit. When He created mankind, Adam and Eve, in Genesis 1:28, God blessed them, and God said they must be fruitful and multiply. I believe when God said, 'be fruitful and multiply, ' it was referring to your gift, the one thing in this world that you're good at.

"A man's gift maketh room for him, And bringeth him before great men."
Proverbs 18:16 (KJV)

So, we can very easily live our lives in *just one season and die unfruitful*. An example is the process to make wine that requires many seasons and processes.

1. *Harvesting*. Grapes are collected from the vineyard when they reach optimal maturity. This is a crucial step, as grapes are the only fruit that can reliably produce enough sugar to make wine.
2. *Crushing*. The grapes are crushed or pressed to extract the juice known as must. This releases the natural enzymes and yeast, which will aid in fermentation.
3. *Fermentation*. The must is allowed to ferment naturally with wild yeast. Fermentation converts the natural sugars into alcohol. The resulting levels vary depending on the climates, cooler climates produce lower levels while hotter climates produce higher levels.
4. <u>Pressing.</u> After fermentation, the grape skins and seeds are pressed to extract the remaining juice and release the wine from solids.

This whole process reminds me of when Jesus says, "I am the vine, and you are the branches."

"I am the vine, ye are the branches: He that abideth in me, and I in him, the same bringeth forth much fruit: for without me ye can do nothing."
John 15:5(KJV)

What amazing scripture, we the people of God are the branches in a comfort zone, until we press in to His presence. 'He that abideth in me' represents to me pressing through the fleshly carnal side of man to abide in Him, and in due season to produce fruit at the harvesting season of your life. At this stage of the process, the grapes are crushed to extract juice, which represents great difficulty, problems, and stresses in life. The Lord is allowing you to be pressed down, this is the process I've been through to complete this book, to produce the fruit of this work. There's a battle raging in the spirit against me, but I know God has given me the victory to succeed. The thing is, we have an enemy, the devil. His sole purpose is to steal, kill, and destroy. He wants to keep everyone in a comfort zone, because you're not a threat to him in a place where you're not producing fruit. He knows your life is not going anywhere; it's stuck in one season. A dry place, unproductive, the spirit of darkness loves dry places, it's like the word, 'lukewarm'. I like my coffee in the morning to be hot, never warm. I believe the Lord is like this with us in our walk with Him.

"So then because thou art lukewarm, and neither cold nor hot, I will spue thee out of my mouth."
Revelations 3:16 (KJV)

First of all, God put a commandment on everyone, from creation in the Garden of Eden, to be fruitful and multiply. From day one, the enemy came to question the Word of God and bring deception so that dominion would be handed over to him. As for me, the Lord spoke to me many years ago, in the early hours of the morning in the book shop, to come out of my comfort zone to produce this fruit of His Word in this book. I started on it straight away, but for many years I've been stuck in a comfort zone of life, working for different employers, with no real satisfaction and fulfilment. I kept silencing this small voice regularly in my head, saying, "You need to finish this work." In prayer recently, I asked the Lord to number my days, because time is short. I then put my hand over this work and asked the Lord to help me finish this great work. So, recently, with real determination to finish, it seemed like there were problems on every side, like something was breaking in the spirit. I asked the Lord in prayer what was going on. He said, "You're going through a *pressing stage*, like with the process of grapes to extract the juice from your life. And even thou it's trying times, be of good courage, because you've overcome the world. Just remain in me the vine, stay connected to me, continue to make room for me every day as you come into my presence."

I believe it's also to do with numbers; God's desire is for us to produce much fruit.

"But other fell into good ground, and brought forth fruit, some hundredfold, some sixtyfold, some thirtyfold."
Matthew 13:8 (KJV)

This is what torments the kingdom of darkness. It's multiplication.

"How should one chase a thousand, And two put ten thousand to flight."
Deuteronomy 32:30 (KJV)

So just one person in prayer can chase a thousand demons, but two people in agreement in prayer can chase ten thousand."

The same with your fruit. God brings His holy fire to your seed and lights it up for His glory. It is a case of releasing it into the waters.

Fermentation. I believe that at this stage, the Holy Spirit is at work converting your fruit into something powerful, changing the whole structure of it, in the kingdom of God, like a weapon in the spirit to destroy opposition. This is also a time of maturity which can only be tested over time, and staying connected to the vine, in daily adoration to the Father.

So, no matter what origin, whether you are black, white, Chinese, Italian, etc. Everyone has a special gift to give the world, with the possibility for it to produce fruit. It's this gift that has been given to you from God from birth.

"A man's gift maketh room for him, And bringeth him before great men."
Proverbs 18:16 (KJV)

So everywhere we go, whether to work or home, travelling, etc., the whole world will stop and make room for your gift, because it's one of the laws of God, which He's put on this earth to work in our favour. I also see this as your inner glory, something beautiful that we all carry inside, that's bursting to come out of the comfort zone of life. Amen.

www.ingramcontent.com/pod-product-compliance
Lightning Source LLC
Chambersburg PA
CBHW061223070526
44584CB00029B/3953